Roger Byrne

Captain of the Busby Babes

A Biography by Iain McCartney

Foreword by Harry Gregg MBE

EMPIRE Publications

EMPIRE PUBLICATIONS LTD
1 Newton Street, Manchester M1 1HW

ISBN   1-901-746-143

Designed and Typeset by
Ashley Shaw and Stuart Fish
and printed in Great Britain
by Redwood Books,
Kennet Way, Trowbridge,
Wiltshire BA14 8RN

To Joy and Roger Jnr

FOREWORD

Thanks For The Memory, Roger

After all these years, I am privileged to be asked to write a foreword to this tribute to Roger Byrne. I have, in my lifetime, been fortunate enough to play with and against some of the greatest players in the history of our great game, no one upheld the highest traditions more than Roger.

Prior to joining Manchester United, I had played against Roger at International level and admired the sublime ability of the man, a player who could defend and attack with the same assured and measured skill. Roger was the finest left back I ever had the pleasure of playing with or against.

After joining Manchester United, I had the pleasure of spending a weekend as guest of Roger and Joy and really got to know Roger. As an opponent he could sometimes appear aloof, but as a guest nothing could have been further from the truth. Here was a man of integrity, warmth, intelligence and sincerity, a man of few words, unless more were required. A leader both on and off the field, he led by example, as his own high standards as a great captain bear out.

In finishing, allow me to repeat myself, Roger - thanks for the memory.

Harry Gregg MBE

ACKNOWLEDGEMENTS

I would like to express my thanks to the following, for their contributions and help Mrs Frances Barclay, Brian Ogden, David Barlow, Albert Kelly, Mrs Irene Joyce, Frank Whitehead, Eric Shorrock, Frank Booth, the late Brian Statham, Sir Tom Finney, David Williams, John Lilley, Alan Aves, Mrs Elizabeth Smith, Mark Wylie, Mike Cox, Mrs Helen Viollet, the late Dennis Viollet, Tom Ritchie, Ivor Broadis, Sir Walter Winterbottom, Don Gibson, Wilf McGuinness, Bill Foulkes, Harry Gregg and, of course, Mrs Joy Worth and Roger Byrne jnr.

Iain McCartney,
Lochvale,
Dumfries

CONTENTS

FROM GORTON TO GLORY

The red-bricked terrace houses of Beech Street, Gorton were similar to countless others strewn across the industrial sprawl of Manchester in the late 1920's.

Gorton itself was a thriving, close-knit community in those somewhat distant days and was home to a youngster whose name would become known and remembered, not just in his local neighbourhood, but across the length and breadth of the country as well as overseas.

It was on February 8th 1929 that Roger William Byrne took his first breath of Mancunian air at 13 Beech Street (now named Wistaria Road), a home he shared with his parents William and Jessie. His father, known to everyone as Bill, worked in the furniture department of Lewis's in Manchester and had a wide interest in sport, ranging from football and cricket to crown green bowling. The latter provided him with the most enjoyment and he was one of the leading lights in the South Manchester Bowling League.

Roger Byrne - Captain of the Busby Babes

His mother Jessie could trace her family connections in the Gorton area back to the early 19th century, when her ancestors had a small farm at Ryder Brow. Her father, Thomas Barlow, was later to become a keen follower of his grandson's footballing career and was a well-known figure himself in the neighbourhood as a member of the High Bank Bowling Club, a founder member of the Gorton Male Voice Choir and secretary of the Gorton A.E.U. Branch.

Near neighbours of the Byrnes in Beech Street were the Ogdens, who had two children, Frances and her brother Brian who was the same age as Roger. Frances, who was a few years younger, still lives at No 27 and recalls fondly what life was like in the area as a youngster.

"We lived on the same side of Beech Street as the Byrnes, having moved there in 1942. Gorton was a busy place in those days, with the engineering works of Peacock Brothers, who built the trains and Gorton Tank who repaired them. We also had Johnstone's Paints at the top of our street, I still call it a street, and when we played outside we always had to watch out for the paint wagons travelling up and down, just in case we got run over. Many's the time the tins would explode as they bumped across the cobbles, providing us with a wonderful sight of all the different colours up in the air, like a coloured waterfall."

Frances's brother Brian continued: "Roger and I were great friends in those early school days, playing football in the streets, with our coats or a jersey for goalposts, and in nearby Debdale Park, where we would also play cricket. Another member of our gang at this time went on to make a name for himself at the other Old Trafford, he was Brian Statham.

"The local baths were another of our haunts and to be honest, it was Roger who taught me to swim during our regular visits.

2

"As we grew older, we ended up going to different schools. I went to one in nearby Varna Street, while Roger went a bit further afield to Burnage Grammar School, so our friendship faded somewhat, although we still saw each other on occasions.

"In those days, you had to do your National Service and I remember Roger joining the RAF when he was about 18. At that time I was serving an apprenticeship, so my call-up was delayed until I was 21. By the time I went in, Roger was coming out, so we saw even less of each other and by the time I had completed my National Service Roger was making a name for himself with United and had a different circle of friends although we did see each other from time to time."

Roger's mother Jessie was one of a family of four and her elder sister Florence lived directly behind the Ogdens in what was then Central Road, but now re-named Carberry Road. Next door to them was the Joyce family and it was into young Irene Joyce's care that Roger was placed on the daily trek to Abbey Hey Junior and Infant School.

"I suppose it was because my family were friendly with Roger's aunt and uncle that he came into my custody for the short journey to and from school, which was only a couple of streets away," Irene recalled.

"He was a very likeable little fellow, well behaved at all times, although a typical boy! Never unruly or one for playing tricks on me as we made our way there and back, but I suppose he realised that the alternative was his mother taking him.

"Each morning I collected him, he would be smartly dressed and it was certainly not a case of no seat in his pants, but made a good footballer.

"Abbey Hey School at that time was old and I mean old. It was known locally as the 'Tin Tabernacle', as the roof was done in corrugated iron, the heating was a stove

3

arrangement with a flue going up to the ceiling, while all the toilets were outside.

"In 1937, however, a new school was opened which was much better equipped. I unfortunately only enjoyed a year in it before moving onto the High School. Roger was able to enjoy a little bit longer in the new surroundings.

"At the 'Tabernacle' there were only two male teachers," Irene continued, "a Mr Archdeacon and a Mr Barber, both of whom would take the boys for football. The former took quite a liking to young Roger and would often carry him around the playground on his shoulders during playtime.

"Compared to some, it was a good school, a happy one, with a good name for scholarship passes and always a good football team. The school eleven would play on a big expanse of waste ground behind the high fence that surrounded the school. Unfortunately, by the time Roger was of age to play in the team I had left, so I never had the opportunity to watch him as a schoolboy.

"Out of school, I would often see him with his friends kicking a ball, or an improvised one, around the streets. Central Road was more than often avoided as a venue due to a mean neighbour who would confiscate all the balls that went over the wall into his back yard, as they were never returned. He really was a nasty devil and I remember that he once came storming out of his house in a blazing temper and banged a boy's head against the wall, which got him in trouble. This failed to stop him nor did it stop the boys from playing in the vicinity of his house.

"As I mentioned earlier, I left Abbey Hey before Roger, moving to an all-girls school, so we did not meet up again as Roger went in the opposite direction to Burnage Grammar, an all-boys school. In any case my family left the area and it was not until his name began appearing in the newspapers in connection with football and Manchester United that I heard of him again.

"You can imagine how pleased I was in later years to say that I used to take Roger Byrne to school even although I never actually saw him play football."

Like most young boys, football played a big part in his life, but he also enjoyed other activities. He was a member of the St James's Church Sunday School and later joined the choir and the Church Lads Brigade where he shone as a talented gymnast.

Upon leaving Abbey Hey Junior School, Roger continued his education at Burnage Grammar School after winning a scholarship, enabling him to enjoy the fundamentals of a good education and also the added bonus of being able to play for Burnage Old Boys Football team at a later date.

At secondary school, he began to show a natural talent for most sport, but drifted slightly away from football, as his father was later to bring to light.

"I always expected Roger to be a cricketer. He played for Burnage Grammar School and was rarely without a bat in his hand. It was not until later that he concentrated more on football."

William Byrne's observations on his son's prowess as a cricketer were certainly not unfounded as, along with a few friends, he joined Denton West Cricket Club. A member of Denton West at that time was Frank Booth, who still recalls the keen youngsters who arrived at the clubhouse with visions of representing Lancashire in the near future.

"It was around the start of the 1947 season that a group of six or seven friends joined Denton West, one being Roger Byrne while another was Brian Statham. At that time Denton West played in the North Western League, having joined just after the war following a name change from Reddish and Gorton Cricket Club.

5

Roger Byrne - Captain of the Busby Babes

"Anyway, Roger was not as good a cricketer as Brian, nor was he as good with the bat and ball as he was a footballer, playing mostly in the second team, whereas Brian was a regular in the first team."

Despite not being a member of the first team, playing cricket gave Roger a year-round sporting involvement for a number of years, with the white flannels and football kit frequently interchanging as summer moved into autumn.

Local Manchester football, like its professional Football League counterpart, suffered during the hostilities of the Second World War, with Burnage High School Old Boys, who had only been formed in 1938, enduring a prolonged break from competitive fixtures.

"After being out of action for most of the war years we restarted in the Lancs Amateur League Southern Section in season 1946-47," recalled Eric Shorrock, the sole surviving founder member of the club, who played for Burnage between 1939 and 1972, mainly at full back.

"It was part way through this season that Roger joined us, preferring in those days to play at inside forward. It was obvious that he was a very talented player, even at 16, but there was also a problem – his size, as he was slightly built.

"Most of the opposition, such as Old Chortonians, Chadderton G.S.O.B., Old Traffordians and Manchester University contained mature men, many of whom although having been out of the game for a period of time and perhaps not entirely match fit, had the physical presence to give anyone a hard game.

"Because of this physical aspect of life in the lower regions of the football world, the selection committee, made up of myself as team captain and three others, had to make the difficult decision of whether to persevere with Roger. After much debate it was agreed to drop him.

"In those days, few of us could boast possession of a telephone, therefore team selection was carried out by informing those selected by postcard, so when no card dropped through the Byrne letter box, Roger knew his fate.

"As we had no second eleven in those days (we field five teams now) Roger had to look elsewhere for a game and subsequently turned out for Ryder Brow in the Manchester Lads Club League. This was a more suitable level of football for a player of his age and build."

A slightly different tale of Roger's Burnage days and departure to Ryder Brow came from former Hon. Secretary of the Burnage Club and a player for over four decades, Frank Whitehead.

"Although I joined the Old Boys after Roger left," began Frank, "the tale of Roger's time at the club is an 'apocryphal' one within our club, aimed at embarrassing Bob Johnson, a man who played an enormous part in the development of Burnage H.S.O.B. when he was alive. However it certainly appears to be based upon fact as ascertained by contemporaries of Bob and Roger.

"Basically, Roger joined us from school and Bob Johnson was club captain, who represented the Lancashire Amateur League at the time. Hence Roger was asked to play full back rather than left wing, since Bob occupied this latter position. Apparently this was not a problem because at school, Roger had progressed to the 1st XI as a full back but at that time Derek Waistall, a rather well-built stopper and much bigger than the young man playing above his years, occupied the defensive role and so Roger was moved to the left wing!

"At that time, however, Bob Johnson was injured, but when he regained his fitness Roger found himself out of the team. As he matured physically though, he was able to move to his favoured defensive role.

"I have always understood that Roger played for

Roger Byrne - Captain of the Busby Babes

Burnage and Ryder Brow simultaneously," continued Frank, "turning out for us on a Saturday and on Sunday he played for Ryder Brow. Certainly, many boys who preferred to watch the professional game on Saturdays played on Sundays, with some strong teams emerging, drawing scouts from professional clubs. Roger was 'spotted' in this fashion."

A BUSBY BABE

As the young Roger Byrne moved through primary school, Manchester City were ruling the roost in Manchester as their Old Trafford neighbours struggled along.

A look through the record books for the pre-war years of the 1930's show the Maine Road side enjoying a Championship success in 1936-37, three years after a Wembley FA Cup triumph, with the likes of Sam Cowan, Eric Brook and Matt Busby enjoying their share of the headlines. United, on the other hand, had to suffer the ignominy of relegation to the Second Division at the end of season 1930-31.

Promotion, as Champions in 1935-36, took United back amongst the elite, only to return to the Second Division a year later. Twelve months later, however, they bounced straight back into the top flight, but the outbreak of the Second World War prevented any further progress from being made. Mancunians became more concerned about the hostilities and the after-dark German air-raids on the vast Trafford Park Industrial Estate than the exploits of Doherty, Herd, Carey or Rowley.

As the city began to recover from the war, life and football began to return to some sort of normality with the Northern War Leagues being replaced with the more familiar divisional fixtures for season 1946-47.

Manchester City, who had been relegated to the Second Division in 1937-38 despite being the highest scorers in the league, sprang back into the big time as Champions, while United, who were now sharing their neighbours' Maine Road ground, completed that initial post-war season as First Division runners-up.

It had been many a long year since United had scaled such heights, but with a new man at the helm in former City half back Matt Busby, the future looked promising.

Between 1946-47 and 1950-51, the Busby-inspired United finished no lower than fourth – in 1949-50, runners-up in all the others – while the FA Cup was won for the first time since 1909 in 1948.

The genial Scotsman from Belshill had transformed an ailing club and United's attacking football brought many plaudits, but it also brought Busby many sleepless nights.

Although one of the top sides in the country with the likes of Jack Rowley, Henry Cockburn, Jimmy Delaney and Charlie Mitten amongst the members of the star-studded team, Busby and his second-in-command Jimmy Murphy were well aware that age was a major factor if any further progress that could be made, with most of the team now in the latter stages of their careers at the top level.

In 1938, the M.U.J.A.C.'s (Manchester United Junior Athletic Club) was formed, with the introduction of 14 and 15-year-olds to organised football having its benefits. John Aston and Stan Pearson of the 1948 FA Cup-winning side were two of the first off the conveyor belt, signing professional forms for United.

A Busby Babe

It was to this level of football that Matt Busby looked to as a means of securing United's future, signing promising schoolboy players from around the country, allowing them to play and grow up together, learning good habits both off and on the field of play.

Along with his backroom staff, they watched countless games at a wide variety of venues, with local leagues constantly scoured in the hope that ninety minutes at some nondescript fixture would see a teenager of promise make it all worthwhile.

A visit to a Lancashire Amateur League Southern Section fixture in 1948 by one of Matt Busby's dedicated staff produced not one but two players whose ability gave the impression that they could perform at a higher level. Both were offered the opportunity to sign amateur forms with United but only one – Roger Byrne – accepted, while his teammate Brian Statham declined the invitation, deciding to stick to his first love, cricket.

It was a decision that Brian Statham never regretted, even though it meant the friends going in different directions at the Chester Road-Warwick Road junction.

"I first met and played against Roger at school," Brian recalled, "when he was in the Burnage Grammar line-up, while I played for Manchester Central High School, meeting twice annually. We later played together for Ryder Brow Boys Club on a regular basis, I played on the left wing, with Roger my partner at inside left.

"He was a natural ball player, with all ball games coming very easily to him. We spent many happy hours playing tennis, table tennis etc as part of a group who met regularly in youth clubs or temperance bars, enjoying sasparella or dandelion and burdock drinks. If it was cold it would be hot Vimto.

"In 1946, half-a-dozen of us joined Denton West Cricket Club upon leaving school, assuming we would all play together in the second team. It did not quite work out as planned, as I never in fact played with the others at all, but went straight into the first team, while Roger and the others had to be content with the second string.

"Our sporting interests had to take something of a back seat," continued Brian, "due to our National Service call-ups, with both of us serving two years in the RAF. Roger could have stayed for a further two as they wanted him to train as a physical training instructor, but he declined their invitation. Surprisingly, he could not get a game in the station football eleven, while I could and he had to be content with outings for the rugby team.

"Back at Ryder Brow we were both offered trials with Manchester United which we both came through successfully. I also went to Liverpool for a trial and again received a positive offer to sign. However, my father thought that football as a career was not a sound proposition, a decision possibly made by the fact that my brother had, as a talented amateur centre forward, broken his collar bone far too many times and this effectively stopped him playing all sports and my father did not want it to happen twice. In the event, my father took considerable persuading to allow me to go to Lancashire County Cricket Club.

"Although we drifted in different directions down the Warwick Road, Roger and I kept in touch and in later years I would join him at United for training prior to the start of the cricket season.

"Roger was an extremely pleasant person and a very good friend. He was level headed and down to earth regarding his own talents which were considerable. My wife Audrey and I remember him with affection."

Brian Statham certainly had no long-term regrets about forsaking United for cricket, as he went on to become a very accurate fast bowler, earning England recognition in 1950-51 and being awarded the CBE in 1966.

A Busby Babe

So, Roger headed down Warwick Road, over the railway bridge and onto the Old Trafford forecourt to begin his career with Manchester United. There is, however, a conflict of dates as to when he actually joined United on amateur forms, with the club giving it as August 18th 1948, while the Football League records show it as a few months earlier in May. It mattered little, the die was cast.

Along with other teenage hopefuls, Roger's first taste of action as a United player was in the Lancashire League side, facing the likes of Goslings, ICI Alkali and Hyde United, or in friendly fixtures similar to that of Christmas Day 1948 when an early morning trip took him to Goodison Park to face a Liverpool County Association XI.

Life as an amateur lasted only a few months before a professional contract was offered and quickly accepted. This was reported in the club minutes dated March 9th 1949: "An amateur player on the club's books, Roger Byrne, has signed professional forms, his terms being as per agreement. The directors approved." The forms had been officially signed five days previously on March 4th. Weekly wages in those immediate post-war days were incomparable to those of the present, with first team players receiving £12 during the season and £10 in the summer. Roger would have been on a fraction of that as he began his footballing apprenticeship.

There were no back page headlines relating to the signing of the 19-year-old from Gorton, overshadowed by another United signing on the same day – Johnny Downie, from Bradford Park Avenue for £18,000, alongside news of Johnny Morris's possible transfer to Liverpool for £25,000. Tucked in beneath those two main stories on the back page of the *Manchester Evening News* of Saturday March 5th was: "Manchester United have signed on professional forms 19-year-old Roger Byrne, a left half back, who has been playing as an amateur in the 'A' team." The *Manchester Evening*

Roger Byrne - Captain of the Busby Babes

Chronicle's Football Pink of the same day carried a mention of United's latest signing in William Fryer's notes on the Manchester League scene, where the correspondent wrote: "United's 'A' team, which dealt a further blow to Goslings' hopes of a hat-trick of championships, is full of talent. Centre half back Jones is a 15½-year-old, 5'11", 11 stone stopper with a bright future. Scottish goalkeeper Young has been coached by none other than the great Jerry Dawson. There is left full back Aston, brother of the first team man to call upon and a brilliant left half back in Byrne."

A month later came promotion to the Central League side to face Everton at Goodison Park. This early taste of football at a higher level came about because Johnny Ball had to step into the league side against Chelsea at Maine Road as full back John Aston was on international duty for England against Scotland.

It was also a Central League debut for Brian Birch, with another youngster, Killin, making only his third appearance at this level, in a team which read: Feehan; Killin, McNulty; Lowrie, Lynn, Byrne; McMorran, Clempson, Cassidy, Birch and Hughes.

Unfortunately, it was not a debut to be recalled in years to come, as the home side won 3-0.

For Roger, the season drew to a close much too quickly as he was beginning to find his feet in the professional game and was encouraged by having had four reserve team outings so early on. The close season, however, enabled him to return to his second love – cricket, and enjoy a few outings with the Denton West Club.

On the eve of season 1949-50 many United supporters had their first glimpse of Roger Byrne playing at left half for the 'Blues' against the 'Reds' in the first team versus the reserves pre-season curtain raiser on August 13th.

The line-ups for this 'trial' match read: 'Reds' - Crompton; Carey, Aston; Warner, Lynn, Cockburn;

14

A Busby Babe

Delaney, Pearson, Rowley, Birch and Mitten.

'Blues' - Feehan; Ball, McGlen; Anderson, Chilton, Byrne; McMorran, Clempson, Cassidy, Buckle and Hughes. Substitutes Lowrie for Byrne, Williams for Anderson.

A crowd of some 17,000 attended this first fixture at Old Trafford for eight years in which the 'Reds' dominated play, winning 5-1. Despite only taking part in the first forty-five minutes of the game, Roger's contribution did not go unnoticed, earning applause and praise for some good work against the more experienced Stan Pearson.

Although commanding a regular place in the reserve side of 1949-50, his 28 appearances were split mainly between left half and outside left, with five at left back. A surprise outing at centre forward came in the Lancashire Senior Cup.

Another youngster with his heart set on a career as a professional footballer was Belfast-born Tom Ritchie. "I first met Roger when I came over to Manchester in 1950," said Tom, "and we played together in the 'A' team, myself at centre forward and Roger at outside left. We also played together in the Central League side after I made my debut at that level against Blackburn Rovers.

"I found him a genuine person and as a player he was a strong and intelligent user of the ball, although he did not think he was captain material when playing as an outside left. I also remember Matt Busby moving Roger from the wing to left back which, at that time, made him very unhappy as he preferred playing up front, although as time went on it became the other way about.

"Although I was to leave United in 1953 as the competition became quite tough with a wealth of talent coming through the ranks, it was a pleasure to play alongside and know Roger."

Season 1950-51 brought a regular place in the Central League side with 31 appearances, scoring twice. Eighteen of those appearances were at left back, one at left half while a dozen found him wearing the number 11 shirt. It also brought his first honour as a United player in the Lancashire Senior Cup.

Having beaten Manchester City 2-1 at Old Trafford in the semi-final on April 18th, following a 0-0 draw in front of 9,000 spectators at Maine Road, Bury were defeated 2-1 (again at Old Trafford) in the Final on May 14th with two goals from Brian Birch. The successful side read – Crompton; McNulty, Byrne; McIlvenny, Jones, Blanchflower; Viollet, Gibson, Cassidy, Birch and Bond.

Manager Matt Busby had encouraged Roger to "keep his eye on the ball" as he continued to try and establish himself in one position rather than be a versatile, play anywhere type. Despite this, Busby had noted the continued improvement and a friendly at Reading on April 25th offered the manager the opportunity to judge how much progress Roger had really made, giving him his first team debut in what turned out to be a thrilling 4-4 draw. The United team read – Allen; Carey, Byrne; Gibson, Chilton, McGlen; Viollet, Pearson, Aston, Downie and Rowley.

The campaign ended on a high note, as less than a month later he was packing his bags to join the established first team stars on a five match tour of Denmark. The name of Byrne only appeared in the first two fixtures, on May 22nd and May 25th, both against a Copenhagen XI, he occupied the left back position in both.

WINGING TO GLORY

Despite the initial breakthrough into the first team at the end of season 1950-51 Roger had to content himself with beginning the new campaign in the reserves, as Matt Busby planned his strategy in a bid to win the somewhat elusive League Championship.

The Central League fixtures kicked off with near-neighbours Bolton Wanderers visiting Old Trafford on August 18th, resulting in a 5-1 victory for United inspired, by Roger who netted a hat-trick, Ritchie scoring the other two.

Beginning the season in fine form and having already appeared in the first team still did not bring him familiarity with the regulars at Old Trafford. One anonymous scribe, writing that "the youngster, having played on the left wing, left half and inside forward might be persuaded to play full back", called him Gerald Byrne!

By mid-November the Central League statistics showed that Roger had played in 15 of the 17 games, scored 5 goals, including his opening day hat-trick, the other two coming against Blackburn Rovers on October 13th in a 3-0 win. The first following an indirect free kick and a pass from Lawrie Cassidy which was driven hard into the net, the second a penalty.

In the club programme, *United Review* No 8 for the visit of Huddersfield Town on November 3rd, Alf Clarke wrote: "Take the Central League side last weekend (versus Barnsley at home). Our wingmen were 17-year-old John Scott at outside right and 16-year-old David Pegg on the left. Whitefoot and Jones were in the half back line, McNulty and Byrne were at full back. Here are the names of six youthful players who are destined for stardom. It is a very pleasant prospect to reflect upon, because the stars must gradually fade out and it is in the excellent replacements available that a team like Manchester United will continue to prosper.

"I have no doubt, in my own mind, that we can look to the future with great optimism. As Matt Busby told the shareholders: 'I don't think there is a boy who has come into our team who has been a failure. We hope to get the elusive Championship, but the most important thing is playing good football. We plan to maintain our high standard. No one will disagree with this ambition'."

November 17th saw Roger make his sixteenth and last Central League appearance of the season. Six days later when checking the team lists for the following day's fixtures he was surprised and bewildered to find his name missing from the reserve sheet. However, a glance at the first team selection showed the reason behind the omission on the former, with the name of Byrne in the line up at left back to face Liverpool at Anfield, taking the place of Billy Redman.

Manchester-born Redman had come into the side the previous season, appearing in the last 12 fixtures of 1950-51, continuing in that position for the opening 18 matches of 1951-52. He was to appear only three more times for United before moving to Bury in June 1954.

The United team for the trip to Anfield on November 24th read: Crompton; Carey, Byrne; Blanchflower, Chilton, Cockburn; Berry, Pearson, Rowley, Downie and Bond.

Alongside Roger on the team coach for the journey along the East Lancs Road was another member of the Central League side who was making his league debut – Jackie Blanchflower, an 18-year-old former Irish Schoolboy International who had joined United in May 1949 signing professional in March 1950.

The United pen pictures from the Liverpool match programme which covered Roger's debut said of the young full back: "Today will be a red letter day for 21-year-old Roger Byrne, who is making his first team debut in Manchester United colours. Roger, who is a product of Manchester junior football, has been with the Old Trafford side for the past three seasons and has made his way gradually from the fourth team to the top grade. He has commanded high praise for his contributions and promising displays in the Central League side this season. Nicely-built and strong in the tackle, he is said to be a real star in the making."

Compliments continued to be paid following the 0-0 draw at Anfield with "Byrne Has Stamp Of Greatness" and "New Boys Win Their Spurs" among the newspaper headlines.

Beneath the former headline the scribe penned the following: "Welcome Roger Byrne. Into a soccer scene almost bare of left backs of international quality steps a 21-year-old debutant with the stamp of future greatness indelibly upon him.

"And it was not a very distant future that Byrne was hinting at as he illuminated the Anfield murk with a first league display glittering with competence and confidence.

19

Roger Byrne - Captain of the Busby Babes

Byrne has served a three-year Busby apprenticeship at Old Trafford as inside left, outside left, left half and left back. Now here is the nearly finished article with a winger's speed, wing half's ball skill and a pair of feet as good as any in English full back play. In two years he will follow John Aston into the England side."

The latter of the two headlines came from the *Manchester Evening Chronicle* where their United correspondent Alf Clarke followed his programme notes of a couple of weeks earlier with further praise. "A game to remember," he wrote, "the debutants Byrne and Blanchflower played a grand game. In his first big match, Byrne kicked admirably with both feet, positioned himself well against Jackson and in at least one instance showed the coolness of Carey himself."

The match itself was a competitive affair with neither side giving much away. Roger was called early into the action to cut out a Liverpool move down the right and his clearance sent Rowley goalward, with his cross headed into Downie's path by Berry, only for the former Bradford player's attempt to go wide.

In the *United Review* the following Saturday, manager Matt Busby wrote: "It is always a pleasure for me to visit Liverpool again, because I had a spell at Anfield and recall many grand days in my soccer career. Now as manager of United, nothing gives me greater pleasure of course for my team to get some reward from a visit to my old club.

"I do think that all the spectators got full value for money last week. To me the interesting features were the debuts of Roger Byrne and Jackie Blanchflower. I feel Manchester United have some of the best soccer prospects in the country and both Roger and Jackie took their chances well. They have been kicking at the first team door for some time."

Unfortunately for Jackie Blanchflower, he found

himself omitted from the team to face Blackpool at Old Trafford the following week, but Roger kept possession of the No 3 jersey, with another 21-year-old, Tommy McNulty as his full back partner playing only his seventh game.

Perhaps it was fortunate for Roger (and Tommy) that Stanley Matthews, along with Mortensen, was missing from the visiting Blackpool line-up as a testing afternoon from the England winger was the last thing he would have wanted so early in his League career. Encounters with the noted outside right could wait.

Both Roger and Tommy McNulty came through the fixture well and their quick, accurate clearances were reported to have caused the Blackpool defence many problems in United's 3-1 victory. Matt Busby must also have been satisfied with their performances as the partnership continued over the following sixteen fixtures.

Roger was later to reflect: "There were a lot of fine young players on the staff and against this intense competition I didn't seem to have much hope. There were indeed times when I regretted the move into professional football. It was only when injuries cropped up that I managed to get into the reserves. However, encouraged by manager Matt Busby, I was patient and just as he promised, my chance came."

United's early season form had been rather erratic, winning nine, losing six and drawing three up to the away trip to Liverpool, but their 3-1 defeat at Portsmouth the previous Saturday was their last in the League until March 22nd, when Huddersfield Town took both points in a five-goal encounter at Leeds Road. In the FA Cup, however, Hull City had caused a major upset on January 12th with a 2-0 victory at Old Trafford. Such a fine run of results could only have helped Roger settle into the rigours of First Division football and the plaudits continued in the local and national press.

Roger Byrne - Captain of the Busby Babes

Following the 5-1 victory over West Bromwich Albion at Old Trafford on December 15th, Alf Clarke called his performance "masterly", while further newspaper space contained "Byrne's form at left back continues to improve so much that the linking of his name with England honours in the near future is no mere flattery."

It was not all praise and five-star performances as Roger began to establish himself as a first team regular and his FA Cup debut in that surprise defeat by Hull City on January 12th brought disappointment along with the early exit.

After giving United an early scare in the 11th minute, when it looked easier for Harrison to score rather than miss after Reg Allen had dropped a cross, Hull took the lead four minutes later with the veteran Carter the inspiration. As Roger and Henry Cockburn backtracked, he found Harrison on the wing with his cross being headed into the roof of the net by Gerrie.

United had the opportunities to draw level but failed to make the most of them, paying for their misendeavours in front of goal by going further behind two minutes before the interval. As a high ball came into the United area, Roger having it covered, moved to head clear only to be pushed by Gerrie, providing Harrison with the goalscoring opportunity which he this time accepted.

A draw seven days later at home to Manchester City, followed by three consecutive victories, the second of which provided Roger with his first real test, took United ahead of Arsenal and Portsmouth, the nearest challengers at the top of the table with a two-point lead.

Sandwiched in between the 2-0 win against Tottenham Hotspur on January 26th and the 3-0 win at Derby on February 16th was a visit to Preston North End's Deepdale, where a 38,000 crowd were eager to see how the relative newcomer to League football would fare against one of the

Roger at 4.... and 13

As a useful pace bowler with Denton West Second XI where Brian Statham began his career.

Roger's registration as an amateur in the 1947 Christie Hospital Charity Cup

CHRISTIE HOSPITAL CHARITY CUP

PLAYERS' REGISTRATION FORM

A.F.C.

Name	Address	Usual Signature	Date of Birth

I declare the above players are amateur players, and are eligible to play under the rules of the competitions.

BURNAGE OLD BOYS   A.F.C.   Hon. Sec.

Date   1947

Macclesfield Town Football Club, Ltd.

Official Programme - 1d.

Macclesfield Reserves defeat at I.C.I. last Saturday may prove a big blow to their championship quest. It was a tale of missed chances in a game which should have provided the Silkmen with two points. As Gosling's secured an easy victory, they are now on level terms and enjoy the advantage of two games in hand. Still, anything might happen between now and the end of the season. I.C.I. have a big programme to fulfil, but they, too, can be serious challengers for the top position.

For the visit of Manchester United " A " this afternoon, Macclesfield will have Holmes at full back and Lyon at inside right. Manchester United " A ", who are a very young side, have a 15-year-old player in Jones at centre half.

Next Saturday, Wrexham will visit the Moss Rose ground in a Cheshire League game.

Manchester League.

Saturday, 26th March, 1949.
Kick-off 3 p.m.

MACCLESFIELD /

R   Arnold   L

Holmes   Howarth

Forster   Powell   Broughton

Jackson   Lyon /,   Baines   Jones   Chorlton

Hughes   Birch   Tidney   Harrop /   Wilson

Buckley   Jones   Byrne

Cowan   Killin

L   Young   R

MANCHESTER UNITED "A" ↷

H. Oldfield & Son, Printers, Mill Lane, Macclesfield. Phone 2507.

One of Roger's first Manchester United appearances - for the 'A' team v Macclesfield - 26th March 1949...

...and in a different kind of United line-up.

Roger at his parents' home in Beech Street, Gorton with Joy and dog Sandy.

Roger shows off the skills that earn him United first team recognition.

Roger's first taste of football overseas comes on United's 1952 tour of America.

Program ...

MANCHESTER-UNITED
vs. PHILADELPHIA

1952 English League Champions

MANCHESTER-UNITED

Back Row: John Berry, Frank Clempson, John Aston, Stanley Pearson, John Downie, Jack Rowley.
Middle Row: John Carey (Captain), Allen Chilton, Henry Cockburn.
Front Row: Tom McNulty, Reg. Allen, Roger Byrne.

SUNDAY, MAY 11th, 1952
KICK-OFF AT 2:30 O'CLOCK
LIGHTHOUSE FIELD
FRONT STREET and ERIE AVENUE
Philadelphia, Penna.

... 25c

Roger drops in on Matt

ROGER BYRNE, 23-year-old England international footballer and captain of Manchester United, paid an unexpected visit to Matt Busby, United's manager, today.

Roger, driving past the Busby home in Wilbraham Road, Chorlton-cum-Hardy, on his way from his Levenshulme home to the United ground at Old Trafford, swerved to avoid a van, skidded across the road and crashed through the garden wall of the house next door to the Busby's.

Hearing the crash, Matt dashed out and helped Roger from the car, and they went on to the United ground together in Matt's car. Roger was only shaken.

Roger's car, badly damaged, ended up on the lawn of the house owned by Mr. J. H. Whitelegg. About 6ft. of wall was knocked down.

The Manchester Evening Chronicle reports Roger's 1952 car crash.

A breakdown van about to remove Roger Byrne's car. In the foreground is the wrecked garden wall.

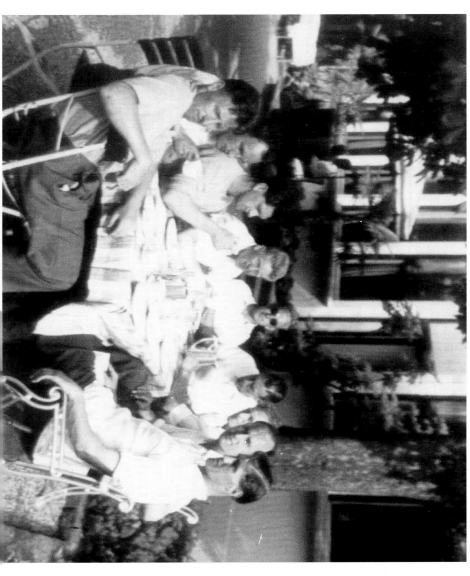

Roger relaxes with England teammates: Bill McGarry, Tommy Taylor, Albert Quixall, Billy Wright, Nat Lofthouse, Tom Finney, Ivor Broadis and Jimmy Dickinson prior to the 1954 World Cup in Switzerland

England line up against Northern Ireland in Belfast, October 2nd 1954.
Team line up – Back Row: Wheeler, Foulkes, Roger, Wood, Barlow, Lofthouse.
Front Row: Matthews, Revie, Wright, Haynes and Pilkington.
England won the match 2-0.

Mark Jones, Johnny Berry, Tommy Taylor, Duncan Edwards, Bill Foulkes, Roger and Liam Whelan prepare to depart for their regular training base at the Norbreck Castle Hotel, Blackpool.

Roger, Matt Busby, Colin Webster, Liam Whelan and Geoff Bent train on the Norbreck Castle Hotel Golf course.

Captain Roger leads United out at Old Trafford

game's outstanding wingers in Tom Finney.

Among those looking forward to the confrontation was United supporter Albert Kelly, who made the journey to Preston with three of his mates from Flixton.

"It was all we talked about on the train journey to Preston that day," recalls Albert. "Roger had settled into the team well, but up until then had not really faced anyone of note and we were looking forward to seeing how he would cope against the more experienced Finney. We all knew what the 'Preston Plumber' was capable of, but we hoped that Roger could handle him and would not receive a runaround.

"By full time, my mates and I realised that we should have had no doubts about Roger's ability as he never gave Finney a look-in and it was clear that United had a player for the future. Having the likes of Henry Cockburn in front of him must have been a big help, but Roger kept Finney well under control, although perhaps on one or two occasions he was just a little bit too robust and enthusiastic."

United continued to hold onto their lead at the top of the First Division, but a defeat against bottom club Huddersfield Town away on March 22nd gave Arsenal the opportunity to narrow the gap, with Roger giving away a penalty in the 3-2 defeat.

A week later, United faced Scottish Division 'A' side Hibernian in a friendly at Old Trafford beacuse their scheduled opponents, Chelsea, were involved in an FA Cup semi-final. Matt Busby surprised the 20,000 crowd by naming Roger at outside left, with John Aston, having enjoyed a spell at centre forward, returning to left back and Jack Rowley moving from the wing into the centre. The change of position, however, only lasted forty-five minutes as Henry Cockburn picked up an injury and went off at the interval with Roger moving back and

Roger Byrne - Captain of the Busby Babes

Ernie Bond coming on as substitute.

It was back to the number three jersey for the long fruitless journey to Portsmouth where a second League defeat in succession created doubts regarding the possibility of landing the Championship, as they were now level on points with Arsenal as the fixtures became fewer.

The defeat gave Matt Busby much to ponder over on the long trek home and the following week a much shorter trip to nearby Burnley saw the manager make six changes, including Roger switching to outside left, with immediate success. The early stages of the game saw Carey and Cockburn contain the Burnley threat of McIlroy and Morris, while Chilton proved a commanding figure in the heart of the visitors' defence. With United well in command of the first half, a long crossfield ball found Roger whose header from eight yards out beat McNulty in the Burnley goal to give United a 1-0 lead and open his scoring account with the club.

It was generally thought that this would give United the impetus required to overwhelm the home side, but Burnley turned on a persistent, aggressive display, snatching a well-deserved equaliser late in the game.

The following day it was the second instalment of a three-part Easter programme, another Lancashire derby, with Liverpool the visitors to Old Trafford. Roger retained the No 11 shirt and was singled out by the media for special attention after scoring twice in United's 4-0 victory, in what was a superb performance, bringing headlines of "Top Gear United Had Championship Look" in the *Sunday Express* and "Liverpool Defence Cut To Pieces " in the *Manchester Guardian*.

Henry Rose of the Express wrote: "The game was a personal triumph for Roger Byrne, a boy who should become one of the team's brightest stars if he has not already arrived.

24

Winging to Glory

"Byrne has previously been extolled as a full back sure to touch the heights, but in this game it was from the outside left position that young Roger captured the imagination and won lots of cheers. There could have been nothing more workmanlike than the way he rocketed the ball into the corner of the net from the penalty spot to put United on the path to victory."

In the *Manchester Guardian*, Don Davies, writing under his pen name 'An Old International' painted a more descriptive picture of the goal. "The penalty was taken by Mitten – fashioned by Byrne, a young left back at present impersonating, and that right well, a genuine outside left.

"The pride with which the populace saw Byrne slam home his penalty was as nought to the gratification they felt when the same young player directed a centre so skilfully that Downie had only to nod and a goal was there."

So 2-0 to United and Roger was soon to make it three, calmly flicking the ball past a prostrate Ashcroft in the Liverpool goal after the custodian had merely parried a terrific shot from Johnny Carey. Liverpool were now clearly beaten, with United having overcome a nervous start, scoring a fourth through Rowley to put the result beyond any doubt.

Easter Monday at Old Trafford brought the hectic holiday programme to a close with the return fixture against Burnley clearly displaying United's title ambitions as they swept the Turf Moor team aside with an emphatic 6-1 win.

By now, Roger was revelling in the outside left role, again scoring a double as United moved two points clear at the top of the table, although they had played a game more than second placed Arsenal.

Once again it was in the second half that they took the upper hand after Pearson twice, Rowley and Carey all came close to opening the scoring in the first forty-five minutes. Rowley netted the first with a gentle tap over the goalkeeper's head, while his inside partner Pearson scored number two from a Byrne centre. Downie chested the ball down and walked it into the net for the third, before Roger stole the show with two fine efforts to give United a 5-0 lead.

Morris scored a consolation for Burnley, but United's five-goal advantage soon returned as Carey headed home a Pearson free kick.

With three games remaining, United continued their title challenge in Lancashire, visiting Blackpool, where they dropped a vital point, holding on to earn a 2-2 draw. As early as the seventh minute they showed their intentions when they had a goal disallowed for offside. However, four minutes later they were 1-0 ahead as Rowley challenged Hayward and Farm, with the ball dropping to Roger to score with ease, his sixth goal in four games.

The Seasiders equalised after nineteen minutes through Mudie and when the half-time whistle blew United found themselves 2-1 behind as Mudie had again pushed the ball beyond Allen in the visitors' goal.

In the dressing room, Roger and his colleagues discovered that rivals Arsenal were two up at Highbury against Stoke, making the second half as crucial a forty-five minutes as they had played for a while.

The Blackpool defence came under tremendous pressure after the restart with Rowley and Carey both coming close. With just over an hour gone, however, the breakthrough finally came when Rowley broke the club individual scoring record for a season with his 26th goal, following a long ball from Henry Cockburn.

Roger was thankful to Cockburn in more ways than one as he almost cost United the game when a bad pass, intended for Downie, was intercepted by a Blackpool forward only for the former England wing half to clear the impending danger.

Winging to Glory

With two games remaining, Chelsea and Arsenal both at Old Trafford, United were level on points with the latter, who had to face West Bromwich Albion away before travelling north to Manchester. They had, however, an inferior goal difference.

Having enjoyed an exciting four-game run at outside left, scoring six goals, Roger had a rather poor afternoon by the standards he had now set himself against Chelsea. On a muddy Old Trafford pitch he was criticised for wasting time and opportunities by shooting from too far out when there was little hope of scoring. Two minutes from the end he had the added misery of missing a penalty which would have given United a 4-0 victory.

At the final whistle, the United players were quick to make their way to the dressing room, not for the steaming hot bath or showers, but to discover how Arsenal had fared at the Hawthorns. The news could not have been better, the Gunners had lost 3-1 and United were now within touching distance of the elusive Championship trophy, as only a 7-0 defeat at the hands of their London rivals in four days time would pip them at the post.

Some 53,651 squeezed into Old Trafford on Saturday April 26th with no doubts in their minds that they would see United crowned Champions. Among them was Albert Kelly who had watched all United's home fixtures and many aways, and even though he was only a teenager at the time, he can still recall much of that afternoon. "As the fixtures became fewer, we began to talk more about United winning the League," began Albert, "and on that particular Saturday there was no way Arsenal would score seven, not even if United had fielded their reserve side.

"I cannot remember much about our six goals or the scorers, although I think Rowley got a hat-trick and Byrne another. Arsenal were not so much beaten but completely outclassed and demoralised.

27

Roger Byrne - Captain of the Busby Babes

"My mates and I always stood on the Popular Side, as it was known then, which is where the North Stand is now. We arrived at the ground around 10 o'clock and immediately made our way to the gates where there were already a few others determined not to miss this particular match."

United were crowned Champions with a 6-1 victory, Rowley scoring three, Pearson two and a solitary effort from a certain Roger Byrne. As Albert Kelly said: "When the first goal went in, I knew that was it and the rest of the afternoon, and night, was one big party."

Amid the descriptive narrative of the afternoon action from Don Davies of the *Manchester Guardian*, he criticised United on only one account, "the excessive feeding of Byrne (who might with advantage copy the selfishness of his senior colleagues) and in the patent neglect of Berry, could United be faulted."

Rowley was man-of-the-match with his three goals, the last of which was a penalty. Whether Roger allowed him to take the kick, giving him the opportunity of completing his hat-trick, or indeed if he had any say in the matter is not recorded, as United brushed the Londoners aside.

United's leading marksman's first was a brilliant drive following a defensive error, the second saw him hooking home a Carey lob. As Don Davies wrote: "In the long history of United there has been no better servant than the 'Gunner'." He also had a hand in two of the others.

As the referee's whistle blew to signify the end of the game and a long campaign, the supporters clambered over the perimeter fencing to proclaim the new Champions. The Beswick Prize Band's effort at playing 'See The Conquering Hero Comes' lasted only momentarily as they were overwhelmed by the onrushing crowd who gathered around the mouth of the tunnel, which was cordoned off by policemen. The crowd were chanting: "We want Carey, we want Carey", who was safely in the sanctuary of the dressing rooms with his celebrating teammates.

On reflection, Roger was more than content with his debut season in the First Division - playing in twenty-four games, scoring seven goals after moving to outside left in the crucial run in at the end of the season. He was later to write: "I was fortunate when I won a regular place in the first team that I was given a lot of encouragement from the crowd, which gave me that added incentive to try just that little bit harder."

In the *Sunday Express* of April 27th, Alan Hoby paid tribute to the new Champions, and under the heading "Busby, Master Switcher", he was quick to acknowledge the contribution of the player he called Busby's 'secret weapon' - Roger Byrne. He wrote: "This 21-year-old kid is goal hungry – and does Matt Busby know it? It was Matt who, a few weeks ago, moved Byrne from left back to outside left at a time when Manchester United lacked goal punch. What happened? Roger has repaid his faith by scoring seven goals in six games, once again proving that Busby is soccer's 'master switcher'."

The last four weeks had been rather hectic not only for Roger but for everyone connected with Manchester United, but there was little time to relax and reflect on the club's first post-war Championship triumph as the bags were soon packed for a twelve-game tour of the United States and Canada, where Roger would find himself once again in the headlines.

The tour began on May 9th, against a USA XI in Keaney, ending in a 4-0 victory with Roger scoring twice, while visits to Toronto, New York, Montreal, Philadelphia, Chicago and Detroit were included in the rather tiring itinerary. It was in Los Angeles, however, that Roger found himself caught up in a fixture that certainly did not fall into the friendly category.

Various select sides had supplied the opposition in the opening games of the tour with exhibition football creating scorelines of 1-1, 6-1 and 10-1. German side Stuttgart had provided the only testing opposition in New York, prior to a double-header against the Atlas Club of Mexico in Los Angeles on the 1st and 8th of June.

The first of the two games began calmly enough with both teams content to pass the ball around and wait for an opening. United's first came in the 30th minute when Stan Pearson opened the scoring firing home from a Byrne corner leaving Gomez in the Atlas goal helpless. Despite going a goal behind, the Mexicans had the best of the first half but could not make any headway against Jack Crompton in the United goal.

Midway through the second half United increased their lead when Roger converted a penalty after he had been tripped in the box by Zetter. The referee's decision to award the kick did not meet with the approval of the Mexican defender as he lifted the official onto his shoulders and dropped him to the ground. At the same time, another Mexican was bouncing the ball off Roger's head and a short, poorly organised riot ensued with Los Angeles County Sheriff's Deputies breaking things up after about fifteen minutes. Needless to say, the original offender, Zetter, was sent off. The rhythm of the game was now unsettled by the unsavoury interruption and when both teams were not involved with each other, they played some good football.

As both sets of players left the field at full time, with United having held on to their 2-0 lead, the ill-feeling resumed with various minor exchanges along with an irate supporter invading the pitch.

Following the disturbing scenes during and after the Atlas fixture, Matt Busby was quite concerned about facing the Mexicans again a week later and considered calling the match off. After much thought and deliberation however he agreed to allow United to fulfil the fixture.

Once again, it was United came out on top winning an exciting ninety minutes by the odd goal in seven, with a Stan Pearson hat trick and one from Roger. Strangely enough, the game passed without a repeat of the incidents that had marred the previous meeting.

It did, however, produce some conflicting details of Roger's performance with Matt Busby later writing in his book *Soccer At The Top* (Sphere Books, 1974): "Atlas were a rough, tough lot. Seeing how things were going, I told Johnny Carey to instruct the team to keep their heads, keep together and keep calm. This he did, but Roger defied him and was sent off.

"I was annoyed about this. I did not like Manchester United players being sent off, though I know before anybody jumps that we have had our share of these unhappy occurrences. I especially did not like my players to be sent off abroad, where club and national reputations suffer more than an individual player's reputation. Nor did I like my instructions or my captain's instructions to be forgotten, even allowing for provocation, of which there was plenty.

"So I had to make my point once more. I was the boss. We would do it my way. I told Roger that he must apologise to Johnny Carey or I would send him home the next day. I would give him two hours to do it in. No more than fifteen minutes later Johnny Carey came to see me to say: 'Roger has been to apologise'.

"So Roger rose in my estimation, high in it though he already was. I knew it was only a lapse into a headstrong state that had caused his dismissal. Now he had shown that he was big enough to apologise."

Surprisingly, this was a complete diversion from the truth, which was reported by United captain Johnny Carey, writing in the *Manchester Evening Chronicle* on June 17th in a regular update of United's overseas adventures.

He wrote: "There is no truth in the report that the referee sent both Jack Rowley and Roger Byrne off the field during our 4-3 win over Atlas. I actually brought Harry McShane on for Roger Byrne midway through the second half, in the second game, because the Mexicans did not like the way Roger was skating past them and alternatively, Roger did not like the methods they were using to stop him. I therefore decided to replace him in order to prevent any trouble which later both Matt Busby and Roger Byrne agreed was the best thing to do."

Roger played in two of the remaining three tour fixtures, but why Matt Busby's recollections twenty-two years later painted such a black picture of his young winger is a mystery which will remain unsolved forever.

TRANSFER SPECULATION

Manchester United kicked off their season as reigning champions with a visit from Chelsea and, prior to the kick-off, two ball boys paraded the trophy around the perimeter of the pitch.

Busby had made no changes to his squad during the close season and the only difference in personnel to the side which faced Chelsea from the one that had finished the 1951-52 campaign was Ray Wood taking over in goal from Reg Allen and Don Gibson wearing the No 6 jersey.

Roger, sadly, did not enjoy the best of starts missing a penalty in United's 2-0 win, his spot kick saved by Robertson after the 'keeper had pulled down a United forward. Don Davies of the *Manchester Guardian* was also critical of Roger in his report of the game. "Byrne in particular came under the lash for over-elaboration and selfishness," he wrote, "chiefly though to those sins he needs must add a missed penalty to fill his cup to overflowing."

It wasn't just the press who voiced a critical opinion of Roger, as four days later at Highbury a vociferous United

33

supporter was heard telling all and sundry within earshot, during the half-time interval that: "Byrne was holding the ball too much last Saturday and also holding it for too long." Unfortunately little went Roger's way in North London to alter the critic's opinion as United lost 2-1, with a similar outcome in the following fixture against City.

Busby decided on changes and Roger found himself re-united with his favoured No 3 jersey, John Aston moving to centre forward for Arsenal's visit to Old Trafford. The 0-0 draw, followed three days later by a 2-0 defeat at Porstmouth, however, did little to convince the United manager that the change had brought any improvement to the team and a week later he was back at outside left to face Derby County where United secured their first victory since the opening day, winning 3-2 thanks to a Stan Pearson hat-trick.

Roger was still struggling to find the form he had shown in the closing weeks of the previous season and against Aston Villa on September 20th, in an exciting 3-3 draw, he was once again considered to have had rather a poor game. Under pressure for much of the game, with little going right, he moved to centre forward, as he had done the previous week against Bolton Wanderers, but soon returned to the wing, much to his disappointment.

His goal-scoring ability also seemed to have deserted him. A simple header went amiss, shooting into the hands of Cardell, the Villa goalkeeper, and with only nine minutes left to play he had a glorious opportunity to give United the lead and possibly both points, but he put the ball past the post with all the goal to aim at.

On the evening of September 24th, his luck took a turn for the better, adding an FA Charity Shield plaque to his collection following United's 4-2 victory against FA Cup winners Newcastle United at Old Trafford. His performance that evening must have pleased him more than that of previous weeks and also given him some added confidence.

The game itself opened briskly with Roger hitting the Newcastle post from twenty-five yards after only three minutes. Soon afterwards he had a second effort cleared off the line by Stokoe. A little against the run of play, the visitors opened the scoring through Keeble, but seven minutes after the interval United were 2-1 in front, Roger having a hand in both goals.

The first, in the forty-eighth minute, saw a Downie-Byrne move create an opening for Jack Rowley to equalise, while four minutes later it was Rowley on the scoresheet once again, following good work by Roger and Don Gibson.

His hard work during the course of the game was rewarded in the sixty-third minute when he accepted a pass from inside right John Downie to score with ease. Four minutes later Newcastle pulled a goal back through Keeble but the game was well and truly wrapped up for United when Rowley set up the fourth for John Downie.

Sadly, the improved performance against Newcastle stood for nothing, as three days later their north-east rivals Sunderland left Old Trafford with both points from a 1-0 victory in front of a disappointing crowd of 28,967.

The following Friday morning, when Matt Busby pinned up his team sheets on the noticeboard for the following day's fixtures, the name of Roger Byrne was a noted omission. His place was taken by 18-year-old John Scott, signed two years previously from Belfast junior football. The Irishman had shown promise in the earlier friendlies against Manchester City and Hibernian, but in his League debut against Wolves he had little to do, other than make a contribution towards Rowley's two goals.

Over the past few weeks Roger had spent much of his free time deep in thought. Although concerned about United's rather indifferent start to the season he was even more concerned over his own performances and held a strong view on Busby's continued practice of playing him at outside left, a position he disliked, preferring to play at full back. Being dropped would not have helped matters much and perhaps prompted Roger into taking some serious action, which surprised Matt Busby and also the United supporters when they opened their evening newspapers.

"United Place Byrne On The Transfer List" proclaimed the *Manchester Evening Chronicle* back page headlines of October 8th. "Manchester United today placed 21-year-old Roger Byrne on the transfer list," wrote Alf Clarke. "The morning after he received his League Championship medal at the celebration dinner, Byrne walked into the United offices and asked to be placed on the list.

"This has been agreed by the club. Byrne's complaint is that he wants to play at left back and not in the attack. He was experimented with at outside left, late last season, scoring many goals for the club in their Championship bid. This season, however, he does not seem to have taken kindly to outside left and was recently dropped. He cannot get the left back position from John Aston and feels he would have a better chance elsewhere."

Many supporters read their newspapers in disbelief and the offices of the *Manchester Evening Chronicle* and the *Manchester Evening News,* as well as those at the Old Trafford ground, were soon to receive many letters and calls of protest from irate supporters.

The news of Roger's request obviously alerted other clubs to his unrest and added interest was shown in United's reserve team fixtures, with Roger the obvious attraction. Burnley were one of the first clubs to closely monitor the situation and their new chairman, Mr Wilfred Hopkinson, witnessed a polished performance by Roger in the left back position in a Lancashire Senior Cup-tie at Goodison Park on October 16th.

Transfer Speculation

With Roger's reluctance to play at outside left, Busby decided that he should perhaps make moves to bring in a recognised wingman. His search took him north of the border to Edinburgh, where he was attracted to the quality peformances produced by the Hibs and Scotland winger Eddie Turnbull. Busby, however, was left disappointed when a bid of £25,000 for the 27-year-old was turned down.

The name of Roger Byrne remained on the transfer list for less than a fortnight, as it was announced on October 16th that he would be continuing his career at Old Trafford. This followed a brief meeting with manager Matt Busby at the ground, during which both parties voiced their opinions and a compromise was reached. The manager also revealed that Roger would be reinstated to the first team at left back for the match at Preston North End in a couple of days' time.

During Roger's brief spell on the transfer list United lost their third successive match, again at Old Trafford, with Stoke City travelling back to the Potteries two points better off following a 2-0 victory. Alf Clarke, in the *Manchester Evening Chronicle* of October 11th was quick to criticise the lacklustre display, writing "United's worst display for years. Scott is not ready for League football" within a report that gave United players little praise.

Matt Busby also realised that it was a poor performance all round and not only did Scott return to the reserves but his selection for the trip to Preston North End showed a total of eight changes to the side which lost to Stoke, four personnel and four positional.

"This looks a better United team," wrote the *Evening Chronicle* correspondent prior to the match at Deepdale, "but how will Roger Byrne fare against Tom Finney?"

The scoreline at 4.45 that afternoon proved that Alf Clarke's fears were completely unfounded, as United recorded an emphatic 5-0 victory, with the England forward having a relatively quiet afternoon.

In the early exchanges, Finney was not given much room by the rejuvenated full back, who kept well within striking distance. On the odd occasion he was caught on the wrong foot, his defensive teammates were on hand to clear any danger. As the game progressed, Tom Finney began to see less and less of the ball and moved to inside right in the hope of bringing some improvement to the beleaguered Preston team who found themselves 4-0 behind after only twenty minutes. By half-time it was 5-0, but in the second forty-five minutes United relaxed letting Preston off the hook.

Although United slumped again at home the following Saturday, 3-1 against Burnley, Roger was happy to be back in his favoured position and began to show some of the form which had been so impressive in the early stages of his career. The team had also turned the corner results-wise as they lost only one other fixture up until January 24th. By then Matt Busby had shuffled his pack frequently, with several new faces appearing in the line-up. Youngsters such as Doncaster and England schoolboys winger David Pegg and Manchester and Lancashire schoolboys inside forward John Doherty made their debuts against Middlesborough on December 6th. Debuts came for St Helens-born Bill Foulkes against Liverpool on December 13th and Eddie Lewis against West Bromwich Albion on November 29th.

Roger's performances, as United began to find the sort of form that won them the League Championship the previous season, were beginning to earn him many plaudits with the previously critical Alf Clarke singing his praises more than most.

Following the 2-1 defeat to near-neighbours Bolton Wanderers on January 24th, he wrote: "Byrne was in international form at left back. Surely an honour will come to this Manchester-born player this season? He brought the

house down once, with a magnificent tackle on Holden."
His one-man crusade to push Roger into the international
spotlight continued seven days later in his *United Notebook*
column under the headline of: "Byrne deserved England
team chance."

"This is a message for the England selectors," he wrote.
"There is a long time yet to the Scotland international at
Wembley and I don't suppose England would be inclined
to change the side which has done well this season. But if
England want a left full back with possibilities of being there
for many more years to come then I advise them to see Roger
Byrne some time.

"Byrne is 23 years of age, that gives him a long time in
normal circumstances to remain in football. He ought to be
considered by England this season and should be an
automatic choice for any 'B' side which may be chosen in
the near future.

"Byrne is the fastest left full back in the country! I feel
confident of that, I rate him England standard now and I
am sure Nat Lofthouse, the England centre forward, will
agree. How ironical that Byrne has stepped in so confidently,
probably to keep John Aston out of an England team at left
back anyway, though England could do worse than select
the two United defenders together. And there is Henry
Cockburn, now back to his best form, he completely
overshadowed England's present left half, Dickinson, in the
recent game against Portsmouth. Is it too much to ask the
FA selectors to see those three United players? They know
how Aston and Cockburn can play, but they have probably
never had the reason to contemplate the future of Roger
Byrne."

Having moved back into defence, the name of Roger
Byrne had failed to appear on the scoresheet during the
opening half of the season and it wasn't until the FA Cup
4th round replay against non-league Walthamstow Avenue

at Highbury on February 5th that he finally broke his duck, scoring a first-half penalty in a 5-2 win.

In February, a month which saw Roger's full back partner Johnny Carey play in goal for ninety minutes at Sunderland, a telephone call to the Byrne household brought the news that he had been selected for the first ever 'B' international match between England and Scotland, to be played on March 11th in Edinburgh.

"Roger has been playing very well indeed," said United manager Matt Busby when informed of the news. "We are all very happy at Old Trafford that he has been selected."

Four days prior to his introduction to international football, he faced the ideal test of his credentials, lining up once more against Tom Finney and, as he had done a few months previously, keeping the England man under close control as United's new signing Tommy Taylor, a £29,999 buy from Barnsley, scored twice on his debut with further goals from Pegg (2) and Rowley in a 5-2 victory.

So it was off to Edinburgh, where many felt that a satisfactory performance would see the name of Roger Byrne included in the full international party to tour South America during the coming summer. He did not let his admirers down, turning in a fine performance which was also appreciated by the fickle Scottish support.

"Byrne and Holden The Stars" proclaimed one of the following morning's headlines and in the report which followed was added: "Although no player stands much of a chance of playing against Scotland at Wembley next month, Byrne of Manchester United and Holden of Burnley at centre forward were the only players not to tarnish their reputations and are worth a place in the England tour party for the trip to America in May.

"Byrne played well against Jackie Henderson, a fast winger from Portsmouth, quite a feather in his cap. More will be heard of him in the international world."

40

Transfer Speculation

His return to domestic football against Burnley at Turf Moor on March 14th promised to be an interesting confrontation between the League Champions and the current League leaders. United could have easily been three goals up in the opening seventeen minutes but the home side kept them at bay and it remained goalless up until the interval.

Roger was having an inspired afternoon, on three occasions holding up strong right wing raids and prompting United attacks, but just as the visitors seemed to be gaining the upper hand Burnley took the lead in the 71st minute, going two in front three minutes later.

Ten minutes from time, United pulled back what proved to be a mere consolation goal, with Roger scoring from the penalty spot after Cummings had handled on the goal line. Despite pressing the Burnley defence right to the end, the equaliser did not materialise.

The chances of regaining the Championship began to look slim, following the defeat by Burnley, as they won only one of their next four outings, with the 4-1 defeat at home by Cardiff City leaving them with little hope of retaining their title. The ninety minutes against the Welsh side was perhaps the worst performance of the season with all four goals gifted to the visitors. Roger was responsible for the third after hesitating on a clearance allowing Tiddy, the Cardiff outside right, to disposess him and loft the ball over the stranded Crompton into the vacant goal.

With the game well out of United's reach and the rain, which was beginning to turn to snow, falling heavily, it was a really miserable afternoon, although United did obtain a consolation goal.

Despite scoring this solitary goal from the penalty spot four minutes from time, Roger's afternoon's work was summed up in one report as "even Byrne's kicking was

41

weak and inaccurate. One of his few constructive kicks was a well-placed penalty."

The only plus points of United's dismal afternoon was the debut of a youngster from Dudley in the West Midlands by the name of Duncan Edwards, a sixteen-year-old of undoubted promise.

With Roger's dislike of being played anywhere but his favoured left back berth, he would have enjoyed a laugh when reading a letter written to Alf Clarke in the *Manchester Evening Chronicle*, which suggested that: "Roger Byrne would be more effective at centre forward due to his speed and shooting power." Much to the United full back's relief Matt Busby did not contemplate such a suggestion.

Three victories, a draw and a 5-0 defeat away to Middlesbrough, brought a somewhat disappointing season to a close, injuries playing a big part in the slump to eighth position with fourteen of the forty-two fixtures lost.

Despite the promise shown in the 'B' international against Scotland back in March, along with the progress made throughout the season, there was to be no full international call-up to join his teammates Tommy Taylor and Johnny Berry on the close season tour of North and South America. Instead, he headed north to Scotland with United to compete in the Coronation Cup competition.

The west coast of Scotland provided an ideal location for the United party's relaxation after a strenuous season, enjoying a week in Troon prior to the competition which, although mere friendlies, held a competitive Scotland-England edge with Rangers, Celtic, Hibs, Aberdeen, Arsenal, Newcastle United and Tottenham Hotspur also involved.

Rangers provided the opening opposition at Hampden Park and much to Roger's surprise he found himself named at outside left as Matt Busby reshuffled the side that had lost 5-0 against Middlesbrough on the last day of the season.

Transfer Speculation

Much to the delight of most of the fervent 75,546 crowd, Rangers took an eleventh-minute lead through McMillan, but they soon found that United were going to be no pushovers despite their indifferent domestic season, with Rowley almost scoring an equaliser nine minutes later.

Despite not having enjoyed his previous outings on the wing too much, Roger did not resent being selected in that position. With the second half barely nine minutes old, he created a scoring opportunity for Stan Pearson to equalise and was involved in the build up of what proved to be the winning goal, scored by Rowley.

The semi-final draw paired United with the other half of the Glasgow 'Auld Firm' – Celtic, but on the day before the match, while playing a round of golf with teammates Jackie Blanchflower, Henry Cockburn and John Aston, Roger recorded a hole-in-one at the 125 yard 8th hole on the Troon Championship course. This saw him having to pay the usual 'forfeit' for such an achievement – a round of soft drinks for his colleagues in the club house.

There was no continuation of the celebrations after the Celtic match, however, with the Scottish side winning 2-1. United were hindered by an injury to Cockburn, forcing Matt Busby to reshuffle his team, with Roger moving from the wing to full back, Aston taking over at centre forward and Rowley moving out wide.

The full-time whistle marked not only the end of a long season, but also the end of an era at United, with the retirement of club captain Johnny Carey. The classy Irishman had joined United in November 1936 from St James's Gate in Dublin for £250 and played some 344 times for the club, appearing in every position except outside left. He had also been a tremendous help to Roger in his progression from the junior ranks at Old Trafford to the brink of international stardom.

BYRNE OF ENGLAND

Season 1953-54 was barely underway, but it soon became obvious that there would be numerous struggles in the weeks ahead. Chelsea had held United to a 1-1 draw in the opening fixture at Old Trafford, while three days later, clad in unfamiliar blue jerseys, an enthralling 4-4 draw had been fought out with Lancashire rivals Liverpool at Anfield.

In the latter fixture, the name of Byrne appeared as a goalscorer for each side in a much talked about ninety minutes. Half time found United trailing 2-1, but with only four minutes of the second half played, the opportunity for an equaliser occurred when Tommy Taylor was brought down in the penalty area by a combined tackle from Hughes and Lambert. Having missed a spot kick in the opening match against Chelsea, Taylor was reluctant to take the kick himself, so the responsibility fell to Roger who placed his right footed shot high into the Liverpool net above Ashcroft to open his account for the season and put United on level terms.

The home side quickly reorganised themselves and two goals in two minutes restored their advantage. The cheering was still echoing around the ground following Liverpool's third goal, scored by Bimpson, when a Liddell centre struck an unsighted Roger, deflecting the ball past Crompton into the United net.

Liverpool soon found themselves on the defensive as United pressed forward and goals from Eddie Lewis and Tommy Taylor earned them a share of the points.

The following Wednesday there was no repeat of a gallant fight back when West Bromwich visited Manchester and the first victory of the season had still to be recorded as the Albion won 3-1!

When the teams were announced for the fourth fixture, Newcastle United at home, a quick glance at the names in the defence produced quite a shock for the man now established as United's first choice full back, as the numbers 1 to 6 read: Crompton, McNulty, Aston, Whitefoot, Chilton and Cockburn. A second glance confirmed that McNulty and Aston were indeed at full back, but moving down through the remainder of the eleven revealed that Roger Byrne had not in fact been omitted as at first imagined, but had been moved to inside right.

Roger was clearly disappointed at once again being moved to a different position and this showed in his overall performance with little impression being made throughout the ninety minutes. With the score line poised at 1-1, he had the opportunity to make a name for himself as the match winner, but hit Cockburn's pass high into the crowd behind the goal, while minutes later saw Simpson hold a shot on the turn at a second attempt.

United were clearly struggling for form, holding a mid-table position, and it was not until September 16th that the first victory of the campaign was achieved, against Middlesbrough away, with Roger returned to his preferred position after just one appearance in the inside right position, scoring from the penalty spot in a 4-1 win. Three days later, it was two in a row for both club and player, with another penalty earning a 1-0 victory over Preston North End at Old Trafford.

Despite the rather inconsistent form there was still a representative call-up in late October with selection for an FA XI to face the Army at St James's Park, Newcastle, casting some light on a rather depressing season to date.

Matt Busby, never one to stand idle, enjoyed the new challenge of friendly fixtures against unfamiliar opposition, allowing him to practise new tactics and players. October 28th saw one of those frequent friendlies, with United travelling north to Kilmarnock to officially open the Ayrshire side's new £3,000 floodlighting system.

During their four-day break at nearby Troon, which followed the disappointing performance against Aston Villa the previous Saturday, when Alf Clarke wrote in the *Manchester Evening Chronicle* of the "shocking exhibition of football", Matt Busby contemplated his team selection on the golf course in between deciding how best to play a particularly difficult hole. Following much debate, and consultation with his No 2 Jimmy Murphy, Busby made five changes to the team which had narrowly defeated Villa, with Crompton, McNulty, Gibson, Blanchflower and Viollet replacing Wood, Foulkes, Whitefoot, Pearson and Rowley.

The slight evening chill did not prevent a crowd of 16,000 from turning out to see how the Scottish part-timers would fare against the famous Manchester United and the home side almost caught the unfamiliar United eleven napping straight from the kick-off, with Murray's shot bulging into the side netting. This, however, was to be one of their few scoring opportunities of the first half as United realised that their brief holiday was over and they were there to play football.

Byrne Of England

In the third minute, Cockburn, in a forward position, attempted an adventurous lob into the Kilmarnock goalmouth from 20 yards out and was surprised to see the goalkeeper slip onto his knees with the ball dropping behind him into the net. It was a rare goal for the United wing half, who unfortunately had to leave the field soon afterwards with a facial injury to be replaced by Duncan Edwards.

Ten minutes before the interval Tommy Taylor made amends for an earlier miss, having finished poorly with only the Kilmarnock keeper to beat, when he put United two up. Accepting a pass from Blanchflower, he quickly side-stepped a defender before evading Brown to push the ball into an empty goal.

Although a friendly, there were numerous hard tackles exchanged, with both trainers taking an active part in the proceedings and as the second half progressed, the visitors wasted an array of goal-scoring opportunities amid the thickening fog. Kilmarnock, however, never looked likely of conjuring up a result and with only five minutes remaining, Viollet scored a third following good work from Taylor and Berry.

This performance gave Matt Busby much to think about on the journey home, with a visit to Huddersfield Town in three days time. The results of late had obviously been disappointing, but should he continue with his established players in the hope that they would soon regain their form? Or should he gamble with those of somewhat limited experience who had performed with much credit at Kilmarnock?

After much deliberation, Busby decided to throw caution to the wind and maintain his youthful line-up with Wood replacing Crompton in goal and Foulkes taking over from McNulty in front of him. Whitefoot and 17-year-old Duncan Edwards took the numbers 4 and 6 jerseys, while

Roger Byrne - Captain of the Busby Babes

19-year-old Jackie Blanchflower and 21-year-old Dennis Viollet kept their places in the forward line at the expense of Pearson and Rowley. The latter did, however, claim the number eleven shirt from McShane, adding some experience to the side.

Huddersfield had begun the season in a promising manner with 22 points from 16 outings, which saw them alongside Wolverhampton Wanderers in joint second place in the League, four points behind leaders West Bromwich Albion. Taking this into consideration, the 0-0 draw played out at the Leeds Road ground could be taken as a favourable result by United. Throughout the ninety minutes the youngsters gave a good account of themselves with their more experienced teammates helping and encouraging them.

Roger, although only 24, was now in his third season as a first team player and was a fitting example to the younger lads, having an excellent afternoon in the United defence. He also showed that he was prepared to break the rules if it would benefit the team, handling the ball to prevent it from reaching an opposition player along with a bit of shirt tugging to subdue the Huddersfield forwards.

Such were his overall performances, speculation was again rife that he could well be selected for the full England side to face Ireland at Goodison Park on November 11th, taking over from Blackburn's Bill Eckersley.

Once again the call failed to materialise, but if there was any disappointment it was never mentioned by Roger, nor did it show out on the pitch, as the rejuvenated United at last found their momentum with only one defeat in the following 12 games, recording notable 6-1, 5-1 and 5-2 victories against Cardiff City, Liverpool and Sheffield Wednesday respectively.

Compensation for the failure to make the full international squad came early in 1954 with selection for

48

the Football League side to face the League of Ireland at Maine Road on February 10th. There was much criticism from the press relating to the fixture as the Irish team were mere part-time players and stood little chance of providing worthwhile opposition to what was almost a full England side – Merrick (Birmingham City); Rickaby (West Bromwich Albion), Byrne; Wright (Wolverhampton Wanderers), Dugdale (West Bromwich Albion), Barlow (West Bromwich Albion); Berry, Revie (Manchester City), Lofthouse (Bolton Wanderers), Sewell (Sheffield Wednesday) and Metcalfe (Huddersfield Town). As it was, the clerks, engineers and foundry workers in the visiting team contributed little in the way of resistance, losing 9-1!

Away from the one-sided performance, along with the poor playing conditions, the national press still found much to write about. George Follows of the *Daily Herald* wrote: "Was it worthwhile? Yes, it was, for the performance of Roger Byrne alone. Manchester United's left back played like a prince. There was no mud beneath his feet.

"He did the job of containing the Irish right wing as casually as though it were the washing-up and still had time to pull Dugdale out of the trouble into which his uncertain tackling led him".

Archie Ledbrooke in the *Daily Mirror* began his match summary: "The story of yeterday's match at Maine Road is of one team hopelessly outclassed by another and of the three local boys making good so to speak. Revie of Manchester City and Byrne and Berry of United were indeed the most prominent players of all." He was to continue: "As for Byrne, he looked what I have said he is for a couple of years, the best full back in England and the best of all the fully-fledged professionals who have come out since the war. His ability to drive the ball hard off the mud was something perhaps some people did not suspect."

Roger Byrne - Captain of the Busby Babes

In the *Daily Express*, Henry Rose devoted most of his column inches to the poor conditions and opposition, but found a few words of praise for the United full back with the observation that "Byrne was ripe for top honours."

The following month saw Roger take big strides towards his first full international cap with selection for the England 'B' squad to face Scotland at Sunderland on March 3rd and West Germany at Gelsenkirchen on the 21st.

His performance against the Scots at Roker Park proved that if one player was a certainty for England's next full international, along with selection for the forthcoming World Cup in Switzerland, then it was Roger Byrne.

George Follows continued to sing Roger's praises from within the pages of the *Daily Herald*, with the heading above his report proclaiming: "Staniforth and Byrne Ideal England Blend." Within the report itself he wrote: "It was a pleasure to record the England 'bests'. Ron Staniforth and Roger Byrne were the best pair of full backs seen in the white shirts of England this season. They played as one, covered beautifully and they were full backs who accepted the old-fashioned responsibility of making goals as well as stopping them."

Alongside Frank Taylor's report in the News Chronicle and Daily Despatch, where he also wrote favourably of the two full backs, Charles Buchan wrote: "Byrne is a great full back and showed that he is ready for the highest honours."

The match in Germany eighteen days later produced another polished performance in front of hundreds of British servicemen who were very appreciative of the 4-0 victory which saw Duncan Edwards line up in front of Roger and steal the headlines from his more senior teammate.

The United duo, however, did not have such an enjoyable ninety minutes three days later at Highbury, with the home side winning 3-0 and Alf Clarke in his *Evening*

Byrne Of England

Chronicle report writing:"I'm afraid that both Byrne and Edwards' disappointing second half form has played them both out of the England team at Hampden next Saturday."

Only the week before, Don Davies of the *Manchester Guardian* had written of the 3-1 victory against Huddersfield Town at Old Trafford: "Byrne gave a faultless rendering of modern full back play. So much so, that his opposite number Burrell was goaded into a few peppery exchanges which did little more than obtain the gentlest of rebukes from the referee." He also wrote that along with Bill Foulkes, Roger felt free to take the sternest disciplinary measures against the opposing wingmen.

The England selectors considered Roger's subdued ninety minutes against Arsenal as a mere hiccup and had no hesitation in naming him for the full England side to face Scotland in a daunting debut at Hampden Park on April 3rd. Duncan Edwards, however, had to wait a little longer for his full England debut.

Turning a deaf ear to the vociferous home support making up the majority of the the 134,000 crowd, Roger made the perfect start to his England career with an encouraging performance in a 4-2 victory for the visitors, despite a mix up with goalkeeper Gil Merrick which resulted in Scotland's second goal late in the game.

The home side took an early seven-minute lead through Blackpool's Alan Brown and if it had not been for Roger's prominence in the England defence, Scotland would have increased their lead on at least three occasions with a clearance off the line along with a couple of timely interventions.

England had drawn level by half-time, before taking command in the second half with a further three goals. A rap on the ankle while tackling Partick Thistle's McKenzie left Roger limping, but nothing could dull the satisfaction of an outstanding full international debut which did much to guarantee further caps.

The England side read – Merrick (Birmingham City); Staniforth (Huddersfield Town), Byrne; Wright (Wolves), Clarke (Tottenham), Dickinson (Portsmouth); Finney (Preston North End), Broadis (Newcastle United), Allen (West Bromwich Albion), Nicholls (West Bromwich Albion) and Mullen (Wolves).

A 3-1 victory against Sheffield United at Bramall Lane on April 24th brought down the curtain on the League campaign, remembered mainly for the introduction of youngsters into the United side, with the likes of Foulkes, Viollet, Edwards, Blanchflower and Whitefoot now permanent fixtures in the first team.

Twenty-seven days after his full international debut, Roger was given the opportunity to further his claim for a regular place in the England side, lining up in a Young England side to face an England XI at Highbury on the eve of the Preston North End – West Bromwich Albion FA Cup Final.

Alongside Roger were Duncan Edwards and Dennis Viollet, while the opposition contained an array of big names in Mannion, Matthews, Lawton and Shackleton to provide a stern test in front of the international selectors. Although the more experienced England XI won 2-1, Roger gave a good account of himself and along with his teammate Tommy Taylor, who missed the Highbury date through injury, found their services were required on the international front for tour fixtures against Yugoslavia in Belgrade and Hungary in Budapest, which were followed by the World Cup in Switzerland.

After a few days rest at home, it was off to Eastbourne for three days' training, where the 31 members of the full international squad, along with the 'B' team were put through their paces. They were then allowed a four-day break at home before re-assembling in London on May 10th for further training before flying out to Belgrade four days later.

Roger's second international appearance ended in a 1-0 defeat against Yugoslavia and he was to recall the events at the end of the ninety minutes more clearly than what had taken place prior to the final whistle.

"Immediately after the final whistle, flames shot up from the terraces, which seemed to be alight from end to end," he recalled. "I fancy that a few hats, coats and eyebrows were singed in that mass bonfire, but no one seemed worried as they were too delighted with their team's victory. It was certainly an awe-inspiring sight."

If that defeat was a disappointment, then his third cap, in the second match of the tour a week later in Budapest, was a complete nightmare.

Why the Football Association chose to play opposition as strong as Yugoslavia and Hungary prior to the World Cup was difficult to understand, especially when the latter had visited Wembley on November 25th 1953 and inflicted the 6-3 defeat which ended England's 90-year unbeaten home record.

The match in the Hungarian capital inspired little confidence in players and public alike for the World Cup competition the following month, as Puskas and company outpaced, out-manoeuvred and out-played the visitors to record a 7-1 victory. Despite being a member of a defence that had leaked seven goals, Roger, the youngest player in the England line-up, received praise for his performance.

Desmond Hackett, writing in the *Daily Express*, lamented: "Only Roger Byrne came through this defeat with any pride. Somehow he found the heart, courage and endurance to go goal seeking when the Hungarians were six up. It was a brand of fighting football that the rest of England had not been able to produce."

53

Roger Byrne - Captain of the Busby Babes

Even the foreign press noted the emergence of a player with a long international career in front of him, as Gianni Brera of the *Gazetta Dello Sport* in Milan was to write after criticising England's style of play: "You should have had the full backs playing wide so they could have gone through more often like that boy Byrne, who was the most excellent player you had. Byrne and Broadis I think were your best."

Three weeks later, the bags were packed once again, Switzerland the destination, to compete in the fifth World Cup tournament, with former United player Walter Winterbottom in charge of the England team. The United representatives in the squad had doubled from that for the two tour games, with Roger being joined by Tommy Taylor, now recovered from muscle trouble. Many felt that Chilton, Wood and Edwards were all worthy of inclusion, but the former was considered too old while the opposite was thought of the latter. Goalkeeper Ray Wood had an injury to blame for his omission.

The format for the 1954 World Cup was rather strange, with four groups of four, two teams in each being seeded. These two teams did not play each other in the group and the top two teams in each group went through into the quarter-finals. England found themselves grouped with fellow seeds Italy, hosts Switzerland and Belgium.

On June 17th, England, with Roger at left back and Tommy Taylor at centre forward, began their quest for glory against Belgium in Basle. Storming into a 3-1 lead, it looked as if it was going to be a winning start, but the Belgians fought back to draw level at 3-3, taking the game into extra time.

Bolton's Nat Lofthouse gave England the lead at 4-3 and that looked enough to earn both points, only for Jimmy Dickinson to head through his own goal to make it 4-4.

Against Switzerland in Berne, a much better defensive performance contributed towards a 2-0 victory and top spot in the group, a point in front of the hosts, who defeated Italy 4-1 in a play-off for a quarter-final spot, as both teams had two points in the group table.

England returned to Basle for their quarter-final tie against current World Champions Uruguay, who had beaten Scotland 7-0 in their final group match. Although they put up a spirited performance, a victory against the South Americans was never on the cards, but the players could hold their heads high despite the 4-2 defeat.

Roger did not enjoy the best of games, with Archie Ledbrooke of the *Daily Despatch* describing his first half performance as "deplorable". Obviously there was disappointment in defeat and the exit from the tournament, but he had enjoyed his hectic few weeks abroad with the International side.

"I did not find it hard to settle with the England side," he wrote a few weeks later. "My full back partner Ron Staniforth was born only five miles from my home, with Jimmy Dickinson always around to help during games and pass on advice. Off the field, Billy Wright was a big help in assisting me to settle in."

"The leisure time brought many enjoyable moments, although one incident, which began with plenty of laughter, ended with a few red faces.

"During a break between the fixtures, we staged a mock boat race across the lake near to our hotel with four people in each outboard motor boat. In my boat were Tom Finney, Ivor Broadis and Ron Staniforth, with everything going well until our motor packed in. At first we thought this was funny, but after drifting for a few minutes an electric storm began with lightning flashing all over the place. Thankfully another boat managed to come out and tow us home."

Former Manchester City and Newcastle United inside forward Ivor Broadis, one of Roger's shipmates, remembers the days on Lake Lucerne. "We used to take regular trips on the lake, but they were not all like the one when the motor gave up on us. Quite often we would travel across the lake in two boats for strawberry teas at a place that was called Stanstaat, or something like that, but those trips were a bit more leisurely and safer than any of our boat races which became quite competitive. Roger was great company and I enjoyed playing with him at international level and, of course, in opposition to him at club level."

CAPTAIN OF THE BUSBY BABES

A footballer's earnings in the mid 1950's were not as mind-boggling as those of the modern game. £15 per week during the season was considered average, while the opportunities of adding to the wage packet through outside commercial interests were few and far between.

As one of the more experienced United players, with just over 100 appearances to his credit plus the added distinction of now being considered an England regular, Roger received an offer prior to the start of the season which would supplement his earnings whilst not interfering with his United commitments. An approach from the *Manchester Evening News* to contribute a weekly column on football in general, rather than a day-to-day account of life at United, was accepted and in the weeks ahead provided talking points for the readers.

A review of the World Cup was the main topic in his debut column in which he wrote: "In my opinion we should not expect any substantial changes in the standard of British football in the coming season and the revolutionary ideas gathered from our experience in the World Cup will take three or four years to materialise." Further down the column he continued: "We are not in the same class as the majority of the continentals and to compensate for this we must make ourselves fitter and faster. Speed and still more speed is what we need." A fair comment, as there did appear to be a distinct gap between British and Continental football both at club and at international level, but it was due more to skill rather than fitness.

With much made today regarding the fitness of the modern footballer, many may find it surprising that Roger and many of his teammates were smokers, as were manager Matt Busby, his assistant Jimmy Murphy and trainer Tom Curry. Unlike today, little was made of the issue which was then considered more of a social thing.

Upon returning from the World Cup, Roger had only a brief break before reporting back to Old Trafford for pre-season training in preparation for another tilt at domestic honours. The campaign, however, could not have got off to a worse start with a 3-1 defeat at Old Trafford by Portsmouth, even though the line-up showed little difference to that which completed the previous season.

Whatever was said by Matt Busby and his assistant Jimmy Murphy following that opening fixture is un-recorded, but it certainly had the desired effect with 4-2 victories over Sheffield Wednesday and Blackpool in the next two outings, followed by six points from home wins against Sheffield Wednesday and Charlton Athletic and an away win at Tottenham. The 2-0 win at White Hart Lane saw United take over the top spot in the League table, a point ahead of Preston North End, Wolverhampton Wanderers and Manchester City. It was, however, neighbours City who were to bring the promising start to an abrupt end at Maine Road on September 25th with a 3-2 win in front of 54,105 supporters.

Roger had still to experience being on the winning side against City in a league fixture and the latest confrontation could be considered his worst of the five he had played in, with a poor free kick going to Revie to set up City's third goal. The press were certainly critical of his performance, with Henry Rose writing in the *Daily Express* that "Roger Byrne was often petulant, often lacked the deportment expected from an international", while a fellow correspondent was quick to bring to the reader's attention that the United full back deserved black marks for two rough tackles on City forwards.

There was no Roger Byrne to be found in the United line-up against Wolverhampton Wanderers the following Saturday, but it was not that Matt Busby had felt it necessary to drop the player following his uncharacteristic display against City. The reason for his omission from the team was his selection to play for England against Northern Ireland in Belfast.

Lining up alongside him were United teammates Ray Wood and Bill Foulkes, both making their international debuts and the United rearguard stood firm against a strong Irish side (which included another United player – Jackie Blanchflower at inside right), helping the visitors to a 2-0 victory.

Surprisingly, it was goalkeeper Ray Wood who stood out from his teammates with some excellent goalkeeping as Ireland pushed the England defence to the limits. One save at the feet of Aston Villa's Peter McParland tilted the game in England's favour.

The pairing of Roger and Bill Foulkes was not considered a success in many quarters with one newspaper reporter going as far as to say that all the English team, besides Wood and captain Billy Wright, deserved to be left out of the next international, with the two United backs always struggling.

October saw Roger's ill-luck take a turn for the better, both on and off the field of play, as United stormed back to the top of the First Division in cavalier fashion, defeating Cardiff City at Old Trafford 5-2, with Tommy Taylor scoring four. Seven days later, in front of 55,966 spectators at Stamford Bridge, they came out on top in defeating Chelsea by the odd goal in eleven.

Both fixtures were epic encounters with Cardiff City surprising the Old Trafford regulars by taking an early lead before succumbing to intense United pressure. In London, it was a completely different ninety minutes, with Chelsea matching United stride for stride, with eight of the eleven goals coming in a thirty minute spell. Tommy Taylor added a further two goals to his tally but was upstaged by Dennis Viollet, who claimed a hat-trick.

Although this was only his third full season as a First Division player and he was only twenty-five years old, Roger had already begun to make plans for when his career would come to an end. He had no inclination for a managerial or coaching position, but took an interest in physiotherapy, studying at Salford Royal Hospital, where the Charge Nurse for Roger's ward was David Williams of Eccles, who remembered his days with his well-known student.

"My ward had Casualty, Orthopaedic, ENT and Cromaxillary cases," began David, "and I remember Roger joining us as a student. Normally a physiotherapy course took three years, but because of Roger's footballing career he was allowed to do his course over six.

"The patients loved him as a person and not just because he was a famous footballer, but I suppose this did create a bit of interest around the wards. He was very skilled in his duties, showing the same determination here as he did on the football pitch, and I have no doubt that at the end of his studies he would have made an excellent physiotherapist.

"I seem to recall that he brought one of his England caps to the hospital, where it was kept safely in a glass security case in the physiotherapy department."

Another member of the Salford Royal Hospital staff at that time was Elizabeth Smith, who recalled: "Our time together at Salford Royal was not on a regular basis, as Roger was a part-time student, which was no mean task, undertaking a six year course.

"Several times Roger appeared on the wards where I was in charge of physiotherapy treatment and football was never discussed, even although my father, Tom Curry, was the Manchester United trainer. Roger never made any reference to his full-time career with United or England and he was always keen to do anything, and I mean anything, that was required for the patients and their treatment. I found him very easy to get on with.

"I had actually seen Roger play many times before I met him, as my husband and I were keen Manchester United supporters. Not many full backs could catch those nippy wingers who thought that they could give defenders a run around, but Roger was a master at this type of play and it was always a delight to see him catch and overtake them, turning and passing the ball back up the field."

Being an international footballer may have impressed the patients, especially the young boys, but made little difference to his fellow students, one of whom was Joy Cooper who lived in Tennyson Road, Droylsden. "We all knew who and what Roger was when he joined us," recalled Joy, "but were not impressed in the slightest, as we did not follow football in a serious manner. Roger, however, enjoyed this type of environment as he wanted to be treated just like any other student.

Roger Byrne - Captain of the Busby Babes

"The Salford School of Physiotherapy in the 1950's was sited at Salford Royal Hospital. The students attended lectures at the school for part of the day, while the rest of the day they treated patients under the supervision of qualified physiotherapists.

"The school and the physiotherapy department were totally separate and the students worked on the wards and in the physiotherapy outpatients departments of Salford Royal and Hope Hospitals, but mainly the former."

Twenty-one year old Joy had become a senior student at the hospital after leaving Fairfield High School, where her sporting interests centred around hockey. "I had enjoyed playing hockey and represented the school and my house team," Joy happily recalled, "and strangely, my position was left back.

"As a young girl, my uncle Albert Wetherall used to take me on occasions to watch United, but I must admit to having no real in-depth interest in the game as a whole and was not too impressed by the presence of a professional footballer in the class."

Roger, however, must have made some sort of impression on the young senior student, as two months later they made up a foursome with two other students, Pete and Ena Ryder who were close friends of Joy at the time, attending the Hospital Christmas Ball. After this, they began to go out together on a regular basis.

Another Annual Staff Dance is recalled by Elizabeth Smith. "One year, it was held at the Fallowfield Hotel, Manchester and I can remember Roger going as Joy's guest and my husband Norman went as mine. Roger had to obtain special permission to attend as it was on a Thursday night during the playing season.

"Anyway, at one point during the evening the band leader announced that Roger Byrne would present a spot prize, without seeking his permission. This caused him more embarrassment than annoyance, as he was in the company of eminent surgeons and medical staff. Such was Roger Byrne the man."

On December 11th a bout of carbuncles forced Roger to miss United's 4-2 victory against Burnley at Turf Moor, his place taken by yet another of Busby's youngsters from the Central League side, 22-year-old Salford-born Geoff Bent, who was making his League debut.

The following Saturday he returned to the fray for the long haul to Portsmouth, but by the end of a goalless ninety minutes he must have wished that he had remained in the more familiar surroundings of Manchester. Judging by his performance, a rather inept display, the illness of the previous week must have taken more out of him than he expected. It was one of his poorer outings, Harris the Portsmouth winger often beating Roger for speed, something that few could boast of being capable of doing, while his clearances were also too haphazard.

Speed was a part of Roger's game where he did excel. Many wingers of that era would push the ball past the full back and beat him for speed before crossing the ball into the penalty area for the oncoming forwards. Roger, however, was an exception to the rule as he could match any winger in the game for speed, even making the two outstanding exponents of that position in the 1950's, Tom Finney and Stanley Matthews, appear ineffective when facing United.

As the calendar changed from 1954 to 1955 United suffered a mixed bag of results, including a 2-0 defeat at Maine Road in the FA Cup that did not help their chances of domestic success. A run of three defeats in a row, the first against Manchester City 5-0, at Old Trafford, next Wolverhampton Wanderers 4-2, also at home and tnen Cardiff City 3-0 at Ninian Park, at the end of February, finally ended any such aspirations.

Roger Byrne - Captain of the Busby Babes

The fixture at Ninian Park on February 26th saw the end of one era and the beginning of another, which in Roger's case helped overshadow the disappointing defeat. The line up against Cardiff City – Wood; Foulkes, Byrne; Gibson, Jones, Whitefoot; Webster, Viollet, Taylor, Edwards and Pegg – showed only one change to that which had slumped against Wolves three days earlier, with 22-year-old Mark Jones taking over the No 5 shirt from Allenby Chilton.

Thirty-seven-year-old Chilton had been sent off in the FA Cup defeat against City and was due for suspension, but had for some time considered retirement and asked to be left out of the Cardiff line-up. After much debate he finally decided that the time had indeed come to hang up his boots. A run of 175 consecutive games for United, which had begun on March 10th 1951, had come to an end. Shortly afterwards he moved to Grimsby Town, where he decided to continue playing as well as taking on the managerial duties.

Manager Matt Busby had lost a commanding figure in the centre of his defence as well as a notable captain, but he had no hesitation in appointing Roger as Chilton's successor, a popular decision with players and supporters alike.

Surprisingly though, Roger was not so popular on away grounds, receiving much abuse as he combined his defensive talents with a fine degree of gamesmanship. Many considered him big-headed, but he simply read the game superbly, making everything look easier than it was. He always contributed 100% in effort to each performance and would never resort to foul play in order to defeat an opponent.

"Roger was the ideal choice as Busby's link between himself and the team," his full back partner Bill Foulkes was quick to point out. "He did not possess the physical strength or presence of Allenby Chilton, who was a real hard man, but he was quick to help any of his teammates and as time went on he was also quick to voice his opinions to Matt if the occasion arose. Exchange could become quite heated between the two, but they did have the perfect working relationship and had great respect for each other.

"I had joined United in March 1950 from St Helens Boys Club as a part-timer, continuing my work at Lea Green Colliery and I immediately became friends with Roger, although as a newcomer to the club I was 23 and nearer to Roger's age than the likes of Duncan Edwards or David Pegg.

"As a part-timer I used to train Tuesday and Thursday evenings, but occasionally we would have practice games at Old Trafford on a Tuesday morning. After the first of those that I was involved in, where I played against Roger, funnily enough, as I had been put into the reserve side at outside left, he asked what I was doing later. When I replied 'nothing', he suggested that we went for some lunch. Glad of the company I was happy to accept his offer and off we went to the Ping Hong in Oxford Road. This became something of a regular occurrence after the Tuesday morning practice games and I was always grateful to him for taking the time to make me feel welcome at the club and help me settle in."

Roger had his own views on being asked to captain United and was later to write: "Following in the footsteps of such eminent leaders as Johnny Carey, Stan Pearson and Allenby Chilton was certainly an honour, while playing under the captaincy of such players you cannot fail to learn and improve your football.

"Obviously the captaincy of a team is not just a case of running out first from the dressing room and spinning a coin. I remember on my first tour with United in Denmark, I was playing my second game for the first team and we were facing formidable opponents in a combined Copenhagen XI, which included five of the Danish international side. They were awarded a free kick two yards in front of our goal and being so inexperienced I did not have a clue what was expected to be done. Johnny Carey, who was captain at that time calmly walked to the ball and directed the rest of us onto the goalline and we prevented a goal from the resulting kick.

"After the game I made a point of asking quite a few of the team what they would have done if they had been captain and they surprised me by answering that they did not know. From then on I paid special attention to the captain's role just in case the honour ever came my way and I would then at least know what was expected of me."

But what was the new captain of Manchester United like as a person and a player? Bill Foulkes offered the following assessment: "He had a fiery temper and occasionally you could see him becoming really annoyed. However, he never ever lost his cool during a game or did anything stupid.

"He was a quiet-spoken individual and you would never hear him shout. To be honest, I do not think that he could shout! Without the need to raise his voice, he could organise the team brilliantly and always got the best out of his players.

"There were odd occasions when he had verbal exchanges with the boss, but no one ever got the better of Matt, not even Roger. There was a great respect between the two that was built up over the years. If any of the players had a problem or a grievance of any kind – money was a popular item on the agenda – then Roger would be asked to approach Matt. But as I said, the boss always had the last word and Roger would always return empty handed.

"As I was a part-timer, I never had the opportunity to mix socially with Roger except for our Tuesday outings, mainly due to the fact that I did not spend too much time at the club. Occasionally, however, there would be a party at someone's house on a Saturday night, with most of the players and their wives or girlfriends coming along. More often than not, Matt and his wife Jean would also be in attendance. The strange thing about such nights, or any club night out come to think of it, when the boss was there, when he got up to go home that was the end of the party.

"I do remember one occasion, though, when I was out with Roger and believe me it was quite an experience. We had both been selected for an England training session, along with Ray Wood and as Roger had a car, the only United player to have one at that time, he said he would drive us down to Henley, I think it was.

"Well, Ray was in the back of the Morris-Minor 1000 with me in the passenger seat and I can remember heading south at 68 mph, which believe me was fast in those days. Up and down those winding roads we went, as there were obviously no motorways at the time and I can remember thinking that we were never going to get there in one piece. Fortunately we eventually arrived there in one piece and we were able to take part in the training without any ill-effects.

"Roger was a clever player, an excellent reader of the game. You would never see him dive into tackles and certainly never see him head a ball unless it was completely unavoidable. He used his speed and would always be in the right place at the right time, cutting out a pass to the winger before it got anywhere near him.

"The likes of Finney and Matthews never liked playing against him as they enjoyed receiving the ball and running past the full back. They couldn't do this when facing Roger as he could outrun them and any other winger that he might come up against.

"His speed was used to its full advantage and he

became possibly the first overlapping full back. If he was ever caught out up front, he had no difficulty in getting back to defend."

Not having enjoyed the best of his exchanges with Roger over the years, what did Tom Finney think of the United defender? "I have numerous recollections of Roger as I played not only against him, but also in front of him on many occasions," recalled the Preston forward.

"We had numerous tussles and I have to confess that he was an outstanding full back and very difficult to play against as he possessed terrific pace along with two good feet, although it must be said that his left was the better of the two.

"I found him to be an excellent reader of the game and a very good technical player. When we were in opposition, he pitted his skills against yours every time, always keeping you on your toes and making things as difficult for you as possible. It was, however, always a pleasure to play against him and of course with him on international duty for England where I got to enjoy his lovely personality.

"Without a doubt, he was certainly one of the best full backs I played against."

With the final link in the 1948 FA Cup-winning chain now broken, the average age of the team had dropped quite a bit. For the match at Preston on March 26th, which saw the debut of yet another talented youngster in the frail form of nineteen-year-old Liam Whelan, it was only twenty-two.

It was a foul on the young Irishman by Preston defender Marsden which earned United their first penalty of the season, resulting in Roger's low shot into the Preston net securing a 2-0 victory. The United side read – Wood; Foulkes, Byrne; Gibson, Jones, Whitefoot; Berry, Whelan, Taylor, Edwards and Scanlon.

The following Saturday, there was no Byrne or Edwards in the United line-up, due to England duty at

Captain of the Busby Babes

Wembley for the Home International fixture against Scotland. This was the Dudley youngster's full international debut and both players gave a good account of themselves in England's emphatic 7-2 victory.

By April 9th, following a 1-0 defeat at Leicester, in what was a rather physical encounter during which Roger suffered a cut head, United slumped to 8th position in the table with 39 points from 36 games, 10 points behind leaders Chelsea. The Londoners, however, had played three games more.

Despite winning three and drawing two of the final six games, including a 2-1 victory over Chelsea on the closing day of the season, United were unable to prevent the Stamford Bridge side from claiming their first Championship in 50 years, finishing the season in fifth position, still five points behind.

As in the previous year, there was no opportunity for a rest until the end of May due to friendly fixtures with both club and country. Three days after defeating Chelsea, Roger was lining up against Aarhus in the first of a four-game tour of Denmark. He was only to take part in three of these fixtures, however, as along with teammate Duncan Edwards he left the United party to join England for friendlies against France in Paris, Spain in Madrid and Portugal in Oporto.

CHAMPIONS OF ENGLAND

By 1955, the Byrne family had moved from their home in Gorton's Beech Street to Erwood Road in Burnage, while Roger's romance with Joy Cooper continued to blossom.

"Since that first date, we continued to see each other on a regular basis," said Joy, "although our physiotherapy studies and Roger's football did sometimes limit the amount of time we could spend together. Our nights out varied quite a bit, from the theatre and cinema, to local pubs with occasional visits to the Cromford Club, which was a regular haunt of United players and the Dixon Arms if we were feeling a bit flush. We left the likes of the Plaza Ballroom in Oxford Road to the younger players.

"Some of our nights out could be quite cheap though, as all the United players had passes to get into the Opera House for nothing, while my father was involved with ABC cinemas so there was also free admission there if a film came along that we wanted to see.

"I was given credit at various times for quietening

Roger down, but he was not the rebel that he was sometimes made out to have been. He was, however, a very positive and determined individual who knew where he was going, working hard to get there. Neither did he suffer fools gladly nor allow anyone to criticise United as a team or any of his fellow teammates. When I first met Roger, he spoke very little about his ability as a footballer even although he was a talented player. In fact, he used to say that the only reason United signed him was because of his Irish surname and that they assumed that he was a Roman Catholic."

Prior to the start of the 1955-56 campaign United faced a testing ninety minutes, which would stand them in good stead for the months ahead, when they faced a Great Britain XI at the Firs, Fallowfield on August 8th. The match was played behind closed doors, and with only the press granted admission, police stood guard at all points of entry to prevent the general public from viewing the game.

Unfortunately for United it was not the ideal preparation for the coming season which was just over a fortnight away as the Great Britain side won 6-2, giving Roger and his fellow defenders a testing time.

The two teams for this fixture read: United – Wood; Greaves, Byrne; Whitefoot, Jones, Edwards; Berry, Blanchflower, Taylor, Viollet and Scanlon. Great Britain – Kelsey (Arsenal) – substitute Fraser (Sunderland) at half-time; Sillett (Chelsea), McDonald (Sunderland); Blanchflower (Tottenham), Charles (Leeds), Peacock (Celtic); Matthews (Blackpool), Johnstone (Manchester City), Bentley (Chelsea), McIlroy (Burnley) and Liddell (Liverpool).

The season itself did not get off to the best of starts either with only eight points gained from their opening eight fixtures, including single goal defeats away at Manchester City and Sheffield United.

Roger missed the 3-1 victory over Luton Town at Old Trafford on October 1st due to an international outing

71

against Denmark in Copenhagen, while three days later he appeared at right back in a friendly at nearby Bury. This sudden switch materialised because Bill Foulkes was unable to secure army leave. Geoff Bent stepped into the vacant left back position for what was a rare first team appearance and combined well with Roger, assisting United to a 5-1 win at Bury and again in the League fixture that followed against Wolverhampton Wanderers, when United earned two thoroughly-deserved points in an exciting 4-3 encounter.

October 15th saw Roger revert back to his familiar No 3 shirt for yet another feast of goals – a 4-4 draw at Villa Park, but it was only for one game as international duty beckoned once again. Many felt that the recent switch to right back might have had some bearing on his international place, but the FA selection committee had no such qualms and Roger lined up against Wales at Cardiff to earn his fifteenth cap.

A return visit to Cardiff seven days later, this time on League business, saw a Tommy Taylor goal settle a tough, testing ninety minutes, a result which took United into top place in the table, although second-placed Sunderland were only a point behind with two games in hand. Blackpool were also in a challenging position, so much so that by mid-November the Seasiders were top, as United could only draw 1-1 at home to Arsenal and failed to return with anything from Bolton, where the home side won 3-1.

The seaside resort did not only provide opponents in the championship chase, but it also became a popular training camp for United, Matt Busby and his first team squad being regular visitors.

John Lilley was a young football-loving supporter back in those mid-fifties days and fondly remembers United's numerous visits. "It wasn't just United who enjoyed the bracing sea air and the opportunity to train in a different environment,"recalled John, "as you could often find two or three teams staying at the popular Norbreck Hydro up on the North Shore. The hotel had its own golf course which the players frequently used and surprisingly this was also used as the training area.

"As young lads, we spent a lot of time out at the Norbreck and United were the most regular visitors. Perhaps this had something to do with Matt Busby having a flat in nearby Cleveleys. My friends and I were keen autograph collectors and always hung around the hotel when teams were there. One day, when United were in residence, I can remember Roger Byrne's black Morris-Minor breaking down in front of the hotel and he asked us if we could push it round the back to the garage. Not needing to be asked twice we quickly got behind the car and after pushing it to where he wanted it, we were rewarded with as many autographs as we required. Ten times for me, some of which I still have today.

"I can also recall Tommy Taylor coming out of the front entrance one day dressed in only a pair of swimming trunks with the intention of walking down to the sea. Unfortunately for him it was much colder than he thought and as soon as the outside air hit him he let forth about half-a-dozen expletives which certainly shocked me. Roger Byrne, however, gave the impression of a quiet but firm personality and looked every inch the captain of the side and also an international player."

Blackpool was not only an ideal place for training, but also an enjoyable location for the players to relax. On one occasion and one occasion only, did things go a bit far, as Dennis Viollet was to recall. "One evening Matt Busby told us that we could go to a show, but stressed that he wanted us back by 11 o'clock at the latest. So off we went in high spirits to see Ted Heath's Band, who at that time were a big name in the showbusiness world and played the type of music we all enjoyed.

73

Roger Byrne - Captain of the Busby Babes

"As the show progressed, it soon became obvious that it was going to overrun its scheduled time and if we wanted to listen to all of the concert then the manager's curfew was out the window. David Pegg, Tommy Taylor, Duncan Edwards and myself had a little consultation along the row and the unanimous decision was to stay put. Not only did we watch the rest of the show, but the Band also played a few encores making it even later in finishing and by the time we all found taxis and got back to the Norbreck it was one in the morning.

"As we tiptoed into the silent, and what we thought was a deserted lobby, like a bunch of errant schoolboys, we suddenly saw trainer Tom Curry sound asleep on a chair in the corner. Obviously he had been waiting up for us. Anyway, still in high spirits someone scribbled a note saying: 'Don't wait up for us', placing it on Tom's lap before disappearing silently upstairs.

"Despite the late night, we were all up as normal and onto the sands for training the following morning without the night before being mentioned. On our way back, however, Tom was asked: 'What time's lunch?' To which he replied that we would have little appetite for food once the Boss had spoken to us and that he wanted to see everyone in the hotel right away.

"We sat like schoolboys awaiting their headmaster until Matt entered the room, slamming the door behind him. He was furious to say the least as he set about us, telling everyone that they were a disgrace, letting not only ourselves down but also the club and our supporters. He ended by threatening to drop everyone if we ever stepped out of line again. Needless to say he was never taken up on his word."

Although now an England regular, there was speculation that Roger's place in the line-up was under threat from Brighton's Bill Langley, but it was simply newspaper talk and he retained his place for Spain's visit to Wembley at the end of November.

By the end of December it was becoming quite a tussle at the top of the First Division between United and Blackpool, with the latter having taken over the top spot following United's 3-2 defeat at Portsmouth on the 10th of the month. A 3-0 defeat at Charlton on the 27th fortunately didn't prove to be too much of a disaster, but the scoreline itself caused a few raised eyebrows as the Londoners had suffered a 5-1 trouncing at Old Trafford the previous afternoon, Roger getting his name on the scoresheet.

This was only Roger's second goal in twenty-seven League games, the previous one coming against Chelsea on November 19th. It should really have been three, but he blotted his copybook during the 4-1 defeat of West Bromwich Albion on Christmas Eve by failing to score from the penalty spot. His initial kick, following Millard stopping Dennis Viollet's goalbound shot with his hand, easily beat the Albion keeper but was disallowed due to a United player enroaching into the area. Once again Roger beat the keeper but could only stand and watch as the ball bounced off the crossbar and behind for a goal kick.

On the final day of 1955 the name of Manchester United re-appeared at the top of the table following a pulsating 'derby' against Manchester City at Old Trafford, watched by 60,956. Thousands were locked out as goals from Tommy Taylor and Dennis Viollet gave United a 2-1 victory over their rivals.

In the mid-fifties period it was not uncommon for supporters travelling to Old Trafford on match days by public transport to find themselves in the company of their heroes as owning a motor car was still a luxury, one that few players enjoyed.

Roger was one of the few who did not rely on a Manchester Corporation bus coming along, owning a

Roger Byrne - Captain of the Busby Babes

Morris-Minor he had purchased, after a lengthy search, from a United supporter who lived in the Lake District.

Matt Busby had often spoken to his players regarding the need to be careful when driving, despite the scarcity of cars around the ground, as even a minor knock could deprive him of a player for an important fixture. His worst fears were realised one chilly January morning, as Roger drove along Wilbraham Road, Chorlton-cum-Hardy, en route for training at Old Trafford.

Without warning, a delivery van turned abruptly in front of him, causing the United captain to swerve quickly to avoid an instant collision. Impact with the van was somehow avoided, only for the beloved Morris-Minor to skid across the road and crash through the garden wall of the neighbouring house to the Busbys, ending up on the front lawn.

The immediate impact was clearly audible in the Busby household, causing disruption at the breakfast table, which was quickly forgotten when Jean Busby informed her husband that the driver was unhurt and that he happened to know him. After the initial shock of being told the identity of the unfortunate, Busby helped his shaken captain from his car, which had suffered the only damage along with the six-foot wall, and took him to training.

"When they arrived later than usual for training, Matt looked a little white," Dennis Viollet was to recall, "and in fact looked more shaken up than Roger. Needless to say that for the rest of the morning we pulled Roger's leg unmercifully, asking him if he was going round after training with bricks and cement to rebuild the wall and suchlike."

Despite being First Division pacesetters as the season moved into the second half, United were not beyond experiencing off days, when their performances could be considered, at best, very ordinary. Such a ninety minutes followed the closely-fought encounter against City in what should have been a routine FA Cup third-round tie against Bristol Rovers.

The 35,872 crowd who packed Bristol's Eastville ground witnessed an inspired performance by the home side, who performed well above their Second Division status to earn a much deserved 4-0 victory.

Roger would remember this cup upset as possibly his unluckiest game in a United shirt as nothing seemed to go right for him throughout the ninety minutes. Early on, he was shaken following a goal mouth mix up and not long after Rovers had taken the lead he was in the thick of things at the opposite end. David Pegg was pulled down (not for the first time) just outside the area and Roger slammed the resulting free kick into the Bristol net. The United players were quick to congratulate their captain, but just a little too quick, as jubilation turned to dejection as the referee disallowed the goal, maintaining that the kick had been indirect.

"Prior to taking the kick, I asked the official if the kick was direct or indirect and he specifically said it was direct," a clearly upset Roger was to state, "but there was nothing I could do when he surprisingly disallowed the goal."

The match failed to improve for the disappointed captain, who was later badly winded, taking the full force of a Petherbridge shot and resumed play only after treatment. In the closing stages he went down on his knees to head clear from Meyer and from the resulting corner was adjudged to have handled on the line with Wood beaten. Bradford scored goal No 4 for Bristol Rovers from the spot, ending a miserable afternoon for both captain and club.

This early cup exit allowed Busby and his team to concentrate on the League. The Reds now led the First Division by six points from Blackpool, following a 2-0

77

victory over third-placed Wolves at Molineux, on February 18th, but the Seasiders continued to pose a threat, having the benefit of a game in hand while Wolves were now nine points behind.

The *Manchester Evening Chronicle* ran a 'Player of the Year' poll, where readers voted for their favourites, who need not be local performers. Back in early December the Wolves and England captain Billy Wright held down the No 1 slot with some 12,216 votes. Duncan Edwards was his nearest United rival in 8th position with 11,419, while Roger had just made it into the top 15 with 10,019.

The poll now showed a much different picture in the week ending February 17th, with Roger having received the most votes during the preceding seven days, moving up to eighth spot with 19,261 votes, 905 behind City's Bert Trautmann who was now in top spot. Duncan Edwards was third with 19,930.

One person who certainly would not have voted for Byrne was Aston Villa's Smith who found himself on the receiving end of one of Roger's tackles which sent him off the pitch and into the perimeter fencing during United's 1-0 victory on February 25th.

March opened with a 4-2 win at Stamford Bridge as the season slowly eased to its conclusion. Seven days later, Cardiff City caused some concern at Old Trafford by hanging on for a 1-1 draw with Roger's 49th minute penalty earning United the point following a forty-yard dash by Viollet which ended with Sullivan outpacing his colleagues and bringing the United forward down.

A second consecutive 1-1 draw confirmed that the pressure of contesting the Championship for so much of the season was beginning to tell, spreading as far as the captain where the cool approach to taking penalties crumbled against Arsenal at Highbury, when his spot kick flew at least five yards over the bar.

Champions of England

As the month drew to a close, a 5-2 victory over Newcastle United at Old Trafford with goals from Viollet (2), Pegg, Taylor and Doherty, followed twenty-four hours later by a 2-0 win at Huddersfield, gave United a seven-point lead with only three games remaining, although second-placed Blackpool had a game in hand.

A defeat for the Seasiders on April 2nd in a Lancashire derby at Bolton and a victory for United at Newcastle would have brought the title to Old Trafford but the bottles of champagne that the Newcastle directors had promised their United counterparts remained uncorked as the 37,395 crowd endured a goalless draw. Blackpool on the other hand kept the title cauldron bubbling by pushing Bolton aside with a 3-1 victory.

By some strange quirk of fate, the fixture list had paired United with their title rivals Blackpool on April 7th, so the team and supporters had to endure a nervous five-day wait for the ninety minutes which would ultimately decide the 1955-56 First Division Championship.

On the day in question, the gates were opened two hours before the kick-off and closed at fifteen minutes to three with a post war record crowd of 62,277 inside, all eagerly anticipating the Championship confrontation.

Roger lost the toss and United kicked off attacking the Stretford End. No one around the tightly packed stadium was quite ready for the drama that was quickly unfolding before them. Seconds after the start, a loose clearance from Jones caused the United defence a bit of bother with Edwards having to give away a throw-in. Matthews quickly took the throw and found Mudie, who immediately turned the ball inside to a virtually unmarked Durie. It was an opportunity not to be spurned and the Blackpool forward had no trouble heading the ball past the diving Wood's left hand to put the visitors a goal up after only ninety seconds.

79

Roger Byrne - Captain of the Busby Babes

United, now up against it, went straight onto the attack and it wasn't long before chances came their way. Taylor produced the first with a neat flick to Viollet whose right-footed shot beat Farm in the Blackpool goal but went inches wide. Next, a free kick on the edge of the visitors' penalty area from Berry saw the ball rebound from a packed defence to Edwards whose lob back into the penalty area was headed against the bar by John Doherty.

Roger created the best chance for an equaliser with a long throw on the left into the Blackpool goalmouth where it just required a flick from Viollet, who was unmarked a few yards out, but he missed the header and the opportunity was lost.

A cross-field run by Perry ended with a tackle from Edwards in the United area, bringing cries for a penalty from the Blackpool players and the few supporters that they had around the ground, but the referee showed no interest in their claims.

At the opposite end, just before half time, the Blackpool goal had to withstand further assault as United continued to press, with efforts from Berry, Pegg and Taylor all being cleared, enabling the visitors to take to the sanctuary of the dressing room still clinging to their slender 1-0 lead.

With manager Matt Busby in Scotland owing to a family bereavement, it was up to Roger and assistant manger Jimmy Murphy to rally the troops and decide on the tactics for the remaining forty-five minutes. There was little need, however, as everyone knew that they had to continue to pressurise the Blackpool defence in the hope that it would eventually yield.

The second half began where the first had left off, with the Seasiders' goal under threat as David Pegg shot over as the ball rebounded from a Gratrix tackle on Taylor, but it was not all one-way traffic with Blackpool always looking dangerous on the break. It was certainly not an afternoon for the faint hearted, with Tommy Taylor receiving a cut head from an aerial challenge, forcing him to leave the field for attention.

Being reduced to ten men failed to stem United's momentum and in the sixtieth minute, during the centre forward's enforced absence, the equaliser materialised. A pass from Berry sent John Doherty through into a scoring position, but just as he was about to shoot, Farm in the Blackpool goal made a desperate but unfair challenge. United had a penalty.

Roger had been the entrusted penalty-taker for some time, but every one of the expectant supporters were surprised to see the equally experienced figure of Johnny Berry step forward to place the ball on the spot. Silence enveloped the Old Trafford arena, as the former Birmingham City man took a few steps back, before placing the ball wide of the helpless Farm. The stadium erupted, United were level.

With everything to play for, the tempo increased as both sides went after the deciding goal. Blackpool came closest first. A Matthews dribble took him to the edge of the penalty area where he was abruptly stopped, while Wood had to produce a fine save to keep the visitors out. United's defence always seemed to be in the right place at the right time.

Despite their enthusiastic endeavour, Blackpool received nothing further in the way of reward as it was United who made the breakthrough ten minutes from time. Berry, always a thorn in Blackpool's side, beat the full back and threaded the ball through to Tommy Taylor only a few yards from goal. The Yorkshireman pushed the ball beyond Farm, but Firth made a desperate attempt to prevent the ball crossing the line. Although he did get a hand to it, the referee allowed the goal to stand.

Roger Byrne - Captain of the Busby Babes

Blackpool, to their credit, continued to make a game of it but Roger and his defensive colleagues stood firm until the final whistle. United were Champions.

Jubilant scenes followed on the terraces and more so in the dressing room where the champagne corks popped in unison. Taking time out from the mass celebrations, Roger said: "To say I am a proud captain tonight is to put it mildly. I can hardly realise the Championship trophy is really ours at last and that the months of tension since we took the lead last December are over.

"Blackpool were worthy opponents. We never underrated their challenge and could not take anything for granted. But we United players were not only fighting for the title today, we were pulling out our best for the man who has done the scheming and worrying for us – our manager, Mr Busby. What a pity he couldn't be here to share this hour of triumph."

A week after adding a second Championship medal to his bulging trophy cabinet, Roger had to miss United's penultimate fixture of the season, a 2-2 draw against Sunderland, due to international duty at Hampden Park, winning his 18th cap against Scotland.

Sporting a bandage above his right eye, as did teammate Tommy Taylor, legacies of the previous Saturday's title decider, Roger turned in yet another notable performance despite this minor handicap, keeping Aberdeen right winger Graham Leggett well under control, much to the vociferous complaints of a very patriotic Scottish crowd.

Old Trafford was packed on April 21st for the final fixture of the season, but no one in the 38,417 crowd had made the journey to the oasis in the industrial sprawl of Trafford Park to see the visiting Portsmouth. Nor was anyone entirely bothered about the ninety minutes of football that preceded the presentation of the Championship trophy, the fulfilment of their dreams.

Champions of England

Prior to the kick-off, Roger led his teammates to the centre circle to salute each side of the ground in turn as an appreciation of thanks for their support during the season. The match itself was a rather nondescript 1-0 victory for United, but it was a proud Roger Byrne who stepped forward to receive the shining trophy from Mr Joe Richards, a member of the League Management Committee, as the crowds swarmed onto the Old Trafford pitch.

There were further celebrations to come when the Lord Mayor and Corporation of Manchester paid tribute to United with a civic reception at the Town Hall. Police motorcyclists led an open-topped coach from Old Trafford to the Town Hall with thousands of cheering supporters lining the route as Roger and the rest of the team held the trophy aloft.

As the procession moved into Albert Square it was greeted by the Police Band, whose playing of 'See The Conquering Heroes Come', was soon drowned out by the noise from the crowd as the players made their way from the coach onto a specially erected platform on the Town Hall steps. The cheers reached a crescendo as Roger stepped forward holding the red and white ribboned trophy high above his head. "We could not have won this Championship without your support," he told the throngs of supporters. "During my brief stay at Old Trafford, never has this club been more United."

One by one, the United players enjoyed the adulation of the supporters packed in front of the Town Hall, before moving inside to join their wives, girlfriends and other guests for a night of celebration.

With the League Championship trophy now secure in the Old Trafford boardroom, most of the players were contemplating a few weeks rest away from it all, but with international fixtures scheduled well into May, Roger was one of the unfortunate few who were going to have to wait for a holiday.

Four days after lifting the Championship trophy, it was across the Irish Sea to face the Irish League at Windsor Park, Belfast. This was the fifth time that Roger had been selected to represent the Football League and, due mainly to the strength of the opposition, had yet to finish on the losing side. Although only 26, he was clearly the elder statesman of the side as he was at least two years older than any of his teammates. This was a major factor in the United captain continuing the role at international level for the first time.

A more daunting task, however, was to come his way on May 9th with a visit to Wembley by Brazil, a side soon to take the football world by the scruff of the neck in a similar fashion to the Hungarians of a few years before. The South Americans found England, with their United trio of Byrne, Taylor and Edwards, a real handful, with the game ending 4-2 in favour of the home side, giving a false impression that it was a closely-fought encounter.

Tommy Taylor captured most of the headlines with two goals in an inspired performance. Colin Grainger of Sheffield United scored the other two as England's forceful play saw them take a 2-0 lead, before two lucky goals allowed Brazil back into the game. Pinpoint centres from Matthews provided Taylor and Grainger with the opportunities to score their second goals as the home side once again took command of a two-goal lead, which should have been increased with two penalty awards. The first, taken by John Ayteo of Bristol City, was saved by the Brazilian keeper while the second was blasted wide of the post by none other than Roger Byrne.

The bags were then packed for a ten-day tour, taking in hundreds of miles, to fulfil three fixtures: against Sweden in Stockholm on May 16th, Finland in Helsinki four days later and West Germany in the Olympic Stadium, Berlin, on May 26th.

84

Champions of England

Although rather tiring at the end of an arduous domestic season, Roger's standards never dropped as he played his part in the three unbeaten games.

The 0-0 draw at the Rasunda Stadium in Stockholm could be credited more to the condition of the pitch rather than the performance of the England side, while Finland provided little in the way of opposition as the 5-1 score-line showed. The final fixture against the World Champions provided a satisfactory conclusion to a long season with England recording a notable 3-1 victory.

Roger's services were called upon a few weeks later, but football boots were nowhere to be seen, although there was no shortage of footballers, as he was asked to be groomsman at former teammate Don Gibson's wedding to Matt Busby's daughter Sheena.

Before Don Gibson's move to Sheffield Wednesday in June 1955, he and Roger had formed a strong friendship which Don was quick to acknowledge. "I became very good friends with Roger in the early days of both our United careers. He had joined United in March 1949, while I had already been there for just over two years. We actually lived only a few miles from each other, but our paths never crossed until we were both at Old Trafford.

"As we were both the same age and playing regularly together our friendship came quite naturally. Tom McNulty and John Doherty also became close friends and we not only went out together at night, to places like the Ritz, but it was not uncommon for the four of us to jog from Old Trafford to my house in Burnage after training for a bit of lunch.

"Our careers ran on something of a parallel from the Colts to the 'A' and 'B' teams, through to the reserves and first team, although I did make the initial breakthrough into the first eleven the season before Roger. Together, we played fifty-odd competitive fixtures together as well as a few friendly games.

"I remember at the end of Roger's first season in the senior side, we were both included in the party to play a number of friendlies in America, something we had been looking forward to for some time. We had both missed out on a similar tour at the end of the previous season but were told then that the club was going back the following summer and we would be on the return trip. As a form of compensation for missing the trip to the States, Roger, myself and a couple of others went to Butlin's in Yorkshire to do some coaching for a fortnight. Although a far cry from America, it was good fun and a nice all-expenses-paid holiday.

"Anyway, when we were on the American tour we managed to upset Matt Busby, which got us into a little bit of bother. For some reason or another we were unhappy with the money we were receiving while we were over there and Roger and I approached Matt in an attempt to obtain a bit more. Let's just say that he was not too amused at our request and shortly afterwards Johnny Carey had a quiet word with the pair of us, explaining that we were the younger members of the party and were receiving the same as everyone else and should be grateful. Needless to say we quickly accepted the captain's reasoning and the subject was never mentioned again.

"Roger was a superb player as well as being an extremely nice person," continued Don, "and we had some great times together. We quite often made up a foursome, Sheena and I, Roger and Joy and I remember one evening in particular, not long after Sheena and I were married, when Roger and Joy came to our house. During the conversation, I commented on the fireside companion set sitting nearby by saying "what a thing to give anyone as a wedding present." Unfortunately I had forgotten that it had came from Roger and Joy!

Roger training at a deserted Old Trafford...

and in a post-match moment.

MANCHESTER UNITED 1955/56
ck Row: Billy Whelan, Jackie Blanchflower, Ian Greaves, Ray Wood, Freddie Goodwin, Mark Jones, Tommy Taylor, Matt Busby (manager)
Front Row: Johnny Berry, David Pegg, Albert Scanlon, Roger Byrne, Jeff Whitefoot, Dennis Viollet, Geoff Bent

MANCHESTER UNITED 1954/55
Back Row: Roger Byrne, Don Gibson, Bill Foulkes, Ray Wood, Jackie Blanchflower, Duncan Edwards
Front Row: Johnny Berry, Tommy Taylor, Allenby Chilton, Dennis Viollet, Jack Rowley

The waiting is over - Roger lifts the Babes' first honour, the 1956 Championship...

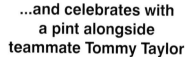

...and celebrates with a pint alongside teammate Tommy Taylor

... and then dinner with the boss.

ROGER BYRNE
Star of the Season

AT the end of each season, "Football Monthly" selects a "Player of the Year." I have no hesitation, this time, in awarding the honour to Roger Byrne, Manchester United left-back.

Not only has he played in every England international, but he has led his side to victory in the League championship for the second year running, to the final of the F.A. Cup and to the semi-final of the European Cup.

Though the fame of John Charles, Wales and Leeds United centre-half transferred to Italian club Juventus, and the exploits of Tom Finney, Preston North End's centre-forward discovery, have commanded a lot of attention, there can be no denying the wonderful stimulus given by Byrne to both the England and Manchester United teams.

His cool, calculated work at left-back, either when his men are in winning mood or fighting to avoid defeat, have been an inspiration. He rarely plays a poor game.

Of course, Byrne has his detractors who assert that he is too inclined to take risks and prone to lose his balance at times.

But one of the reasons why Byrne is undoubtedly the best full-back in the country today is his confidence in his own ability. What appear to be risks—and would be risks to the ordinary player—are part and parcel of Byrne's immaculate style.

The square pass back from the bye-line to his goalkeeper and the bold dash forward to assist the attack come naturally to Byrne, who started his career as a forward and has complete command of the ball.

And if Byrne occasionally resents the attention paid to him or his colleagues, it is because he is so whole-heartedly immersed in the game. That he is the captain of United proves that these rare moments are insignificant.

Byrne is still comparatively young, 27 years of age. The longer he plays, the better he will become. He has the brains to make the best use of his great skill.

Born in Manchester, he has been a United man first and foremost. He has played a conspicuous part in their many successes.

Byrne is not only a quick thinker but very fast on the run. He has the speed to cope with the fastest of modern wing forwards. And the positional sense to limit their activities.

Most important of all, Byrne always uses the ball to advantage. His well-timed clearances have started many England and United attacks from within their own quarters.

With either foot, Byrne places the ball from his full-back position, straight to the feet of his forwards. It is a relic of his youthful days when he put across many accurate centres from outside-left.

Byrne is busy, too, planning for the future. He is training hard to qualify as a physiotherapist and I have no doubt he will become as skilled in this art as he is on the soccer field.

C. B.

Voted Football Monthly's Star of the Season for 1955-56

**United's captain,
a dedicated follower
of fashion,
watches the Babes train**

Roger addresses the crowds in Albert Square with
the 1956 Championship Trophy.

The champions at a celebratory dinner
at Lewis's, Manchester, 1956.

Saturday June 5th 1957 - Roger and Joy are married at St. Mary's, Droylsden. Roger arrived with his best man, Jack Pickles, twenty minutes before the 11 o'clock service to discover a large number awaiting his arrival. Many wore United colours and clutched cameras, while a hopeful few carried autograph books.

Roger and Joy emerge through an archway of football boots carried by Roger's groomsmen: E.Barnes, E.Blinkhorn, H.Henfry, N.Cox and former teammate Don Gibson...

By the time Roger and Joy emerged from the church as husband and wife, following the service conducted by the Rev H.W.Hewitt, the awaiting crowd had increased to a few hundred and required a dozen policemen to try and keep things under control.

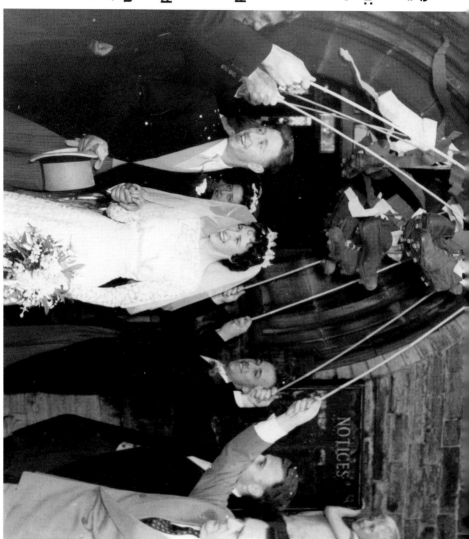

The Babes take off for Europe

United's captain on the rack

Roger, Tommy Taylor and David Pegg soak up the rays in Madr
prior to the European Cup semi-final first leg at the Bernebeu
United lost 3-1 and, eventually, 5-3 on aggregate

MANCHESTER UNITED 1956/57
Back Row: Jeff Whitefoot, Bill Foulkes, Ray Wood, Mark Jones, Jackie Blanchflower, Wilf McGuinness
Front Row: Johnny Berry, Colin Webster, Roger Byrne, Tommy Taylor, David Pegg.

Champions of England

"As I said, Roger was a well-respected figure within the club and Matt thought the world of him, often speaking very highly of him when we were together. After my transfer to Sheffield Wednesday, we still remained close, as I was a frequent visitor to Manchester. I am proud to say that he was a very dear friend and someone I will never forget."

CHAMPIONS OF EUROPE?

Since his appointment as manager of Manchester United in 1945, Matt Busby had not been content to stand around and wait for things to happen. He rarely remained on the touchline, observing training sessions from a distance, but instead pulled on a tracksuit and joined in, showing the players what he required instead of telling them.

He was quick to spot the adaptability of certain members of his playing staff, enabling him to prise that little bit more from his team as he blended them into an attack-minded outfit. Being the best in England was all very well, but there was always room for improvement and the opportunity of proving themselves at a higher level.

The inauguration of the European Cup competition in the previous season caught Busby's imagination, even though the Football League had prevented Chelsea, the 1954-55 League Champions, from competing. When the invitation to compete in the 1956-57 competition arrived on his desk, he explained to the directors how important it was to enter and, after much deliberation, they agreed to back their manager's decision.

Strangely, a letter to Old Trafford from the Football Association said that it could be to the club's advantage to enter the European Cup, while the Football League still refused to give their consent. Busby, however, had no intention of missing an opportunity to widen the horizons and the name of Manchester United went into the draw for the preliminary round on June 30th 1956.

Season 1956-57 resumed where the previous one had left off, with United clicking into gear right away, recording ten victories in the opening twelve fixtures, the other two ending in draws. Despite picking up an injury at Preston in the second match of what was going to be a long campaign, Roger was fit enough to continue leading the team, with the 1-1 draw at St James' Park on September 8th his 200th League and Cup appearance for the club.

September 12th is not a date instantly recognisable and remembered, but it is a notable one in the history of Manchester United as it marked the first fixture in a European competition. The match in Brussels, against the Belgian champions Anderlecht, saw United gain a 2-0 advantage with goals from Dennis Viollet in the 25th minute, after a run from almost the half way line before shooting past Week in the Anderlecht goal and Tommy Taylor with a typical headed goal 15 minutes from time.

Roger and fellow defender Mark Jones had outstanding games, keeping the home forwards at bay. Goalkeeper Ray Wood also kept United in the game with a fine penalty save when the match was poised at 1-0.

At the official after match function, after being presented with a lighter and ashtray mounted on a leather stand and embossed with the Anderlecht club crest, Roger said: "I was extremely happy with the way we played and

89

Roger Byrne - Captain of the Busby Babes

I think we have maintained the prestige of British football and may even have enhanced it. Things might have gone very differently if Anderlecht had equalised from the penalty, that was really the turning point. As things were, Mermans gave us a lot of trouble but there wasn't the craft behind him to create the openings he could use."

Three days later it was back to the bread and butter of League football, with a visit to Old Trafford from Sheffield Wednesday. There was no drop in the standard of play after the European excursion as United swept their opponents aside with Roger in exceptional form.

Frank Taylor, in his match report for the *News Chronicle and Daily Dispatch* wrote: "It was a triumph of top-class teamwork. If I must single out anyone, then I name Roger Byrne as man-of-the-match. Roger has his critics, but his was a streamlined display right out of the top drawer. He had Finney – who can be one of the most dangerous wingers in the game – a helpless prisoner on the touchline.

"Byrne not only kept the Wednesday matchwinner out of the game, but also zoomed up into the attack himself to start the moves which led to the first three goals. There was England class written all over this Byrne display."

United warmed up for the second leg of their European Cup tie with a 2-0 home victory over neighbours Manchester City, but for the visit of the Belgians they had to rent City's Maine Road ground, because there were as yet no floodlights at Old Trafford.

Following a torturous ninety minutes, the Belgians would have preferred to have faced City rather than their rampant tenants of the evening, as United showed little compassion running up a 10-0 score line.

"United Thrash Anderlecht", "United Hand Out Soccer Massacre" and "Busby's Boys Bang In Ten" were just three of the following day's headlines which acclaimed United's devastating victory. Goals came from Viollet (4),

Taylor (3), Whelan (2) and Berry. Roger had a hand in numbers seven and eight, by which time he had pushed so far forward that he was practically playing on the wing.

The momentum continued three days later in front of 62,479 spectators at Highbury, beating Arsenal 2-1 without too much trouble, although Roger almost let the home side back into the game by fouling Tapscott to give away a penalty which Evans converted. United, however, held onto their one-goal advantage to maintain their unbeaten run.

The visit of Charlton Athletic to Manchester on October 6th not only marked a two goal debut by Bobby Charlton, but also stretched the team's unbeaten run to 31 games – 25 in the League – beating Burnley's 1920-21 record. Roger unfortunately missed this milestone in the club's history because he was on international duty at Windsor Park, Belfast.

On October 17th, it was back to Maine Road where the quest for success in Europe resumed with the visit of Borussia Dortmund. There was no repeat of the goalscoring free-for-all that destroyed Anderlecht, indeed the German side gave United a few unexpected problems.

Three goals in front after only thirty-five minutes, it looked to most of the 75,598 packed into City's ground that they were in for another goal feast, but Dortmund, inspired by their goalkeeper Kwiatkowski, began to rally and by the end of the night had pulled the scoreline back to 3-2, with the general feeling of those leaving the ground that a one goal advantage would not be enough to see United through.

Frank Taylor, who only a few weeks previously had sung Roger's praises, was slightly more critical on this occasion , writing: "I blame Roger Byrne, the United skipper, for the slip which started the avalanche of Borussia attacks. In the 70th minute, instead of kicking the ball away, Byrne breasted it nonchalantly down for goalkeeper Ray Wood. Alas, left winger Kapitulski was there first and Byrne held his head in disgust as the ball rocketed into the net." A further defensive error brought the Germans' second goal.

When questioned by reporters after the game, Roger was man enough to hold his hands up and admit to his error, while at the same time answering the criticism with: "Yes, it was a silly mistake on my part, but do none of you ever make mistakes?"

Surprisingly, Roger's performance was once again under close scrutiny in the national press following United's first defeat of the season, 5-2 at home to Everton, who by a strange coincidence were the last side to win at Old Trafford back in March 1955.

One reporter, Don Evans, who attended the match wrote: "Skipper Byrne had his worst outing for many a season, gifting Everton one goal. He put a free kick straight to the grateful McNamara who slammed the ball back across goal to Kirkby and Everton were 2-1 in front."

Alf Clarke, in the *Manchester Evening Chronicle*, was equally scathing in his report: "Byrne could do very little right and this must be about his most unimpressive game of the season."

It was another wet night in Manchester for the battle of the giants as United faced City for the FA Charity Shield trophy at Maine Road on October 24th. The dismal weather and the televising of the game kept the crowd down to 30,495, but they still managed to create an exciting atmosphere.

Considering the opportunities created, United should have won comfortably, but to their credit City managed to keep the scoreline down to 1-0, Dennis Viollet's goal enabling Roger to lift his second trophy as club captain.

The match, however, is perhaps best remembered for the introduction of 15-year-old goalkeeper David Gaskell into the United defence in place of the injured Ray Wood.

Champions of Europe?

United continued to defend the title with determination and no game illustrated this more than the trip across Lancashire to Blackpool on October 27th, when the Seasiders stretched the United defence to the limits.

Having kept a tight reign on the effervescent Matthews for most of the afternoon, Roger let his guard drop in the 53rd minute, allowing the winger to send one of his pinpoint crosses into the area where Mudie headed home. Thankfully for the United captain, a Tommy Taylor header earned United a point with only a minute left to play.

The short journey to Burnden Park, Bolton, a fortnight later, produced the second draw of the season where 'The Tramp', in his match report for the *Bolton Buff*, commented that: "Banks surely disproved that Roger Byrne is the best left back in England", a point that would receive very little backing outside the town's boundary.

Roger, as has been mentioned previously, had his critics, particularly on the terraces at away grounds. Although there were occasions, when his play was not appreciated by opposition supporters, he always played fair although he would revert to gamesmanship if he though it might benefit his team. He was also quick to question refereeing decisions as spokesman for the team if he considered them incorrect. Twice in a fortnight examples came to light in fixtures at Old Trafford, against Wolves and Leeds United.

Against the former, it was very surprising to hear boos drifting around the ground directed at the United captain, as he took the opportunity to slow the game down with a long pass back to his goalkeeper, with United leading 2-0 and the game moving into its last few minutes.

Fourteen days later, against Leeds he was perhaps fortunate to remain on the field of play as he remonstrated rather forcefully with the referee, following the award of a penalty kick to the visitors after Wilf McGuinness had tackled Meek. Before John Charles could take the kick, Roger moved forward to speak with Ray Wood, receiving a further admonishment from the official.

Such incidents did not perturb Roger as he was back to face referee Windle shortly afterwards when Leeds again had the ball in the back of the net. His protests on this occasion were listened to and the goal disallowed.

One person who thought very highly of Roger was United's trainer Tom Curry, who in accordance with the club rules was responsible for the discipline of the players. His daughter Elizabeth Smith recalled one particular incident that her father had told the family about.

"It happened at the Norbrek Hydro Hotel at Blackpool, which was frequently used by the team for special training before a big match. My father was in the lounge with several members of the local and national press, while the players were having their meal in the dinning-room. The head waiter appeared and approached my father to inform him that one of the players had asked for a glass of beer to have with his meal. My father asked the waiter what drinks were on the table and was told that every kind of soft drink was available to the players. The waiter was told not to provide anything else, especially alcohol.

"The player involved was junior and became very vocal, forcing Roger to take him to one side to tell him that he was out of order: 'Tom Curry is in charge and his decision is final.' Roger also told the player that if they had a bad game on the Saturday, it would be all over the papers that Manchester United players were indulging in lunchtime drinking. It was also suggested by Roger that the player immediately apologised to Tom Curry. This he did in front of the sports writers.

"This is an example of the players' respect for Roger as their captain, on and off the field, and also the respect Roger had for club officials."

The return European tie in Dortmund provided Roger

with the ideal opportunity to make amends for his misendeavour of the first leg and he was in fact back to his defensive best with an ice-cool performance, marshalling his teammates through a difficult cup-tie which earned United a creditable 0-0 draw and a place in the next round of the European Cup.

Frank Taylor wrote after the match that Roger, along with Ray Wood and Mark Jones should have been given the freedom of Manchester for their performances, but these three individuals and the rest of the United players would have been happy with another couple of pounds in their wage packets instead.

Following the success on the European front against Anderlecht and Dortmund, the players felt that they had a reasonable case with which to approach Matt Busby in the hope of obtaining a bonus payment.

"It was the very first time that we had all sat down and talked about money," recalled Dennis Viollet, "and because of the big crowds that the games had attracted and the money they had brought in, we felt that we deserved a little extra for our efforts. So, it was decided that Roger should approach Matt and plead our case for a win bonus. It must be remembered, at that time we received only £2 for a win, £1 for a draw and £3 for a match under floodlights in the European Cup.

"Roger must have got his point across to the boss and made something of an impression as he came back with the reply that the Football League would be approached regarding bonus payments and Matt would see what he could do. It was later announced that if we beat our next opponents – Athletico Bilbao – we would receive a £3 win bonus or 30/- (£1.50) for a draw. The payment for playing under floodlights would increase to £5. If we went on to lift the European Cup we would receive an extra £5.

The end of November brought a couple of international

fixtures against Wales and Yugoslavia at Wembley, along with league fixtures against Leeds at Old Trafford and Tottenham Hotspur at White Hart Lane sandwiched in between. Both Wembley appearances produced victories, but in the Yugoslavia match Roger had the unfortunate experience of missing yet another England penalty kick.

Although a defender, deeply involved in the physical confrontations of the game, his injuries were few and far between, much to the relief of Matt Busby. However, a knock in training, forcing a late fitness test prior to the match against Tottenham had a prolonged effect.

He came through the game without much of a problem and also completed the ninety minutes the following Saturday against Luton, but four days later he aggravated the heel injury while playing for England against Denmark at Wolverhampton, forcing him to miss two consecutive matches.

Thankfully, the 3-1 defeat at Birmingham City in the second of those missed outings did little to dent United's title aspirations and by mid-January, following a commanding 6-1 trouncing of Newcastle United at Old Trafford, they were six points clear of Tottenham Hotspur with 48 points from 25 games.

Christmas 1956 brought the official announcement of Roger and Joy's engagement, having made the initial decision a month earlier. This announcement was made while out with a large group of friends at the Dixon Arms, Chelford. The wedding was planned for June 1957.

Prior to the emphatic win against Newcastle, both Roger and the United team as a whole came in for further criticism following the 4-3 FA Cup victory at the northern outpost of Hartlepool.

The Third Division North outfit should really have been on the end of a hiding and with just over half-an-hour played it looked as if double figures could be a possibility with goals from Whelan in the seventh minute, Berry a minute later and Taylor in the 32nd, giving United a comfortable 3-0 lead.

Determined not to go down without a fight, the home side surprisingly fought back to draw level with goals in the 35th, 53rd and 65th minutes, before Liam Whelan put the game beyond doubt fifteen minutes from the end.

Were United becoming too big for their boots? Too big-headed? Did they adopt a rather casual approach against their lowly opponents? Those and similar questions were asked by supporters as United made their way back to Manchester and the more comfortable surroundings of Trafford Park.

Roger had perhaps more fingers pointed at him than any other United player, coming under a scathing attack in the local Hartlepool press. In the *Northern Daily Mail*, their correspondent wrote: "Byrne, of all people, was now adopting 'kick and clear' tactics as 'Pools harried and chased everything in search of an equaliser."

The *Sentinel*, however, was a bit nearer the knuckle in its match summary, including the following: "The astonishing feature to me was the performance of Roger Byrne. The England full back kicked and gesticulated like a raw newcomer to the game as fighting 'Pools, backed by a roaring crowd, threatened to shatter the Babes."

The FA Cup made way for the European Cup and it was certainly not sunny Spain as Roger led United out for the quarter-final first leg against Athletico Bilbao. The falling snow quickly helped to turn the pitch into a mixture of slush and mud, with United struggling against a side that had only been defeated once at home in three years.

By half-time, United were 3-0 down, but during the half- time interval, Matt Busby, Jimmy Murphy and Roger evolved a tactical plan to try and stem the Spanish tide in the second half.

Roger Byrne - Captain of the Busby Babes

Within eight minutes, United had clawed themselves back into the game with two goals from Taylor and Viollet, but this was later to be outdone as poor defensive work saw the home side score a further two goals before Whelan scored what many thought to be a mere consolation effort near the end, as the 5-3 scoreline left United an uphill task in Manchester, where they required four goals to go through on aggregate to the semi-finals.

February opened with a highly emotive Manchester 'derby' at Maine Road, where Roger was clearly the target of the boo-boys amongst the City supporters in the 63,872 crowd. His reception from the Moss Side faithful was not completely due to his position as captain of their dearest rivals, but more in line with a motivated performance in United's 4-2 win, which helped earn two precious points when at times it looked as if the game could be drifting away from them.

"Captain Courageous Bullied The Babes – Booed Byrne Just Loved It" was the headline above Derek Wallis's match report in the *Daily Mirror*, which proceeded to recall, for the benefit of its readers, Roger's Saturday afternoon endeavours. "Say what you like about Roger Byrne. Maybe he does fuss like a maiden aunt. Maybe he does throw out the occasional flash of temperament," began Wallis's report, "but I am saying that Byrne bullied his men out of a second-half slumber and saved a point for Manchester United at Maine Road.

"Here was the captain courageous – a strong man who listened to the crowd's boos and heard a call to action. Here was a captain courageous who listened to two stern lectures from the referee and charged back into the game as if they had been pep talks."

Wallis proceeded to describe how United controlled the game completely until their "cocky streak got a grip" and City began to fight back. "This was the moment when

Byrne stepped in," continued the *Mirror* man, "the longer they booed, the harder he played. He loved it!"

Four days later, on February 6th, United and their supporters made a return trip across Manchester, attracted like moths to the Maine Road lights, for the second leg of the European Cup quarter-final tie.

Never had Maine Road experienced a night like it as United took the game to the Spaniards from the offset, determined to erase the visitors' two-goal advantage. Amongst the feverent 65,000 crowd that night was Brian Turner, who some forty years on has no problem recalling the events of that particular evening.

"I clocked off work an hour earlier than usual," began Brian, "as I knew from the previous ties what it would be like heading over to Maine Road and I was thankful that I did. There were people everywhere, looking for tickets, friends and heading for the turnstiles. Just as I was going through the gate I saw one man give a tout £11 for a stand ticket, such was the desire to be there. Once inside I heard that touts had been selling forged tickets for £5. The noise inside was deafening as United attacked the Spanish goal and more than once I got cracked on the side of the head by a rattle-clacking supporter alongside me."

From the first whistle United went on the attack to try and pull back the needed goals, but were a little bit too eager, missing a couple of good chances early on. Bilbao knew what to expect and whenever possible slowed the game down. They were also calm and well organised in defence giving little away.

As the first half ticked away, it looked as if United were never going to score, but three minutes before the interval came the breakthrough when Dennis Viollet quickly fired the ball past Carmello after an Edwards shot had rebounded off a defender.

Bilbao defended stoutly as the second half progressed

and United pressed forward, but the visitors could do little to prevent Tommy Taylor from levelling the tie on aggregate in the 72nd minute, after twice breathing sighs of relief when 'goals' by Viollet and Whelan were both disallowed for offside.

As the ball hit the back of the net, Maine Road erupted with a noise that would surely have echoed around Manchester. "I had no idea who scored," said Brian Turner. "One minute the ball was in front of the Bilbao goal, the next it was in the back of the net. Everyone around me went wild, many would never have seen their hats or caps again."

Roger mustered his side for the final eighteen minutes, determined that no play-off in Paris would be required, but as the minutes ticked away such an outcome began to look more and more likely.

With only five minutes remaining, those who still had a voice and the power in their lungs urged United forward. Taylor, who had drifted wide to the right, flitted past two Bilbao defenders and as Garay prepared to launch himself into a tackle the England centre forward squared the ball to Berry. The diminutive winger instinctively placed the ball out of the keeper's reach to give United the goal they required.

With only a couple of minutes to go, United very nearly let it slip when a back pass from Foulkes to Wood was badly judged, but thankfully the goalkeeper just managed to get there before the onrushing Bilbao forward.

Upon the final whistle grown men cheered with tears in their eyes and strangers hugged one another as Matt Busby and Jimmy Murphy did a victory jig on the touchline. United were through.

Three days later, Arsenal travelled north to Manchester with visions of becoming the first London side to win at Old Trafford since Charlton Athletic took both points in

October 1938, but the adrenaline and momentum had drifted across Manchester from Maine Road with the Londoners succumbing to a devastating performance from the home side as United swept them aside with a 6-2 victory.

Fixtures were now coming thick and fast and due to the frequency of midweek matches, it was sometimes difficult to maintain the interest and concentration of players as practice games were now off the training schedule. However, physical training in the fully-equipped gymnasium under the main stand at Old Trafford was frequently used, with Eric Evans, an England rugby union international from Sale Rugby Club often in command.

Droylsden-born Evans had joined the Sale club after the war, making his England debut against Australia in 1948 as loose-head prop, but did not become an international regular until 1953. He regularly trained with United during the pre-season weeks and became very friendly with Roger, who took an interest in rugby union, watching Sale whenever possible. The variation that Eric Evans provided in these sessions helped keep the players interested and fit in the vital run in to a dramatic season.

A 1-0 victory over Everton in the fifth round of the FA Cup produced a difficult away tie down on the south coast at Bournemouth, where the Dean Court club made United fight all the way for their 2-1 victory.

Making his FA Cup debut that afternoon was Wilf McGuinness, who recalled the pulsating cup-tie with fondness. "This game sticks in the mind for various reasons, not just because it was my first taste of FA Cup football, but because it emphasised to me not only how good a player Roger Byrne was, but it also brought out his skill as a master tactician.

"Bournemouth had a player called Ollie Norris, who was a complete nutter. There was no other way to describe him. Anyway, he was involved in everything, with an early

101

tackle on Mark Jones forcing the big defender out of the game. Roger quickly assessed the situation and pulled Duncan Edwards back from his centre forward role to take over at centre half. This was without any consultation with the boss. Throughout the game he also helped me along, often switching positions with me to take the pressure off if Bournemouth were pressing strongly.

"But back to this Ollie Norris. He had the infuriating habit of jumping up and down in front of you as you prepared to take a throw-in or a free kick. This piece of gamesmanship came to a rather abrupt end, however, when he tried it on as Roger was about to take a throw-in.

"Leaping up and down in front of Roger on the touch line, he was suddenly holding his face in his hands due to the ball having hit him full in the face. Whether or not it was an accident or deliberate I never found out, but I have my own opinion, and Norris did not do it again that particular afternoon."

The south coast club had shocked their illustrious visitors by taking the initiative in the 35th minute through Bedford and it was not until fifteen minutes after the interval that the equaliser came. Berry moved into the middle, accepted a through ball from Foulkes and as the home defence stood looking for offside, the winger cracked the ball home.

Four minutes later Berry struck again, this time from the penalty spot after Lyons had handled Whelan's goal-bound header. United were a step further on their march to Wembley.

Standing in the way of United's first Wembley appearance since April 24th 1948, when Blackpool were beaten 4-2 in one of the most thrilling Cup Finals for years, were Birmingham City.

Having drawn their two League fixtures prior to their semi-final date, United were certainly not in for an easy afternoon, with many considering the Midland side the more likely to progress into the Final. Roger himself acknowledged that his team faced a tough assignment in a pre-match interview, saying: "We all know we are in for a hard struggle and it will be a vital test that can decide all our hopes. If we get over this one, then I am sure we will land that treble chance."

As the ninety minutes progressed, it became clear that the Midlands side were not going to provide the sterling test that many thought they would and as early as the 12th minute United found themselves in front, a lead they always looked unlikely to relinquish.

Roger began the move which led to that opening goal, slipping the ball through to Pegg who wriggled past two Birmingham defenders before passing to Charlton who in turn found former Birmingham favourite Johnny Berry who shot past Merrick from some 18 yards out.

One minute later United were two in front with the provider of the first, 19-year-old Bobby Charlton, playing in his first cup-tie, leaving Merrick helpless following a cross from Pegg.

"There wasn't much good football in this match," Roger was later to say, "but the little that there was came from United. Bobby Charlton's goal was the turning point. After that we were never really concerned about the result."

Preston North End used United's cup semi-final involvement to their advantage, keeping up the pressure in the Championship race, by defeating Luton Town 2-0 to reduce the gap at the top to a mere three points, although they had still played two games more. United's 2-0 defeat by Bolton Wanderers gave Preston further encouragement, but a 2-1 win at Leeds five days later, while Preston lost at Villa, left things as they were.

April 11th brought not only a vital test for United's treble credentials but also the opportunity for Matt Busby to discover just how good his young side really were, as they travelled to Madrid to face the European Cup holders in the first leg of the semi-final. It was a confident United who travelled to the Spanish capital, unnerved by their opponents stature in the European game.

A member of the squad who travelled to the Spanish capital, as cover for wing halves Eddie Colman and Duncan Edwards, was Wilf McGuinness, who recalled the pre-match relaxation with a rueful smile. "Most of the lads were sitting around the hotel pool, showing little in the way of nerves and I decided to join them as an afternoon in the sun would do me little harm, as I had little chance of playing in the game itself. Coming out of the hotel doors, I spotted a vacant seat right beside the pool and quickly made my way over to it, sat down and made myself comfortable.

"Minutes later, I felt a slap to the side of my head and upon opening my eyes saw the figure of Roger Byrne standing over me looking none too pleased. 'Go and sit somewhere else,' he said in not too friendly a manner, which I did not take too kindly to, thinking it rather rude and bad mannerly, even if he was the captain, just to walk out of the hotel and ask me to get up from my seat, particularly as there were one or two others elsewhere which were not being used. 'Why don't you go and sit on one of the others?' I boldly enquired, to which Roger replied: 'Because this was my seat and I have just been to the toilet.' Needless to say I was not long in moving to one of the other vacant seats amid one or two sniggers.

"Had it been one of the other first team players, Roger would probably not have bothered and sat elsewhere, but to find a youngster from the reserves occupying his seat was just a bit too much to bear. Even though I had played a few games in the senior side, in Roger's eyes I was a reserve team player and he had set rules within the club which we minors had to adhere to.

"One of those club rules that the youngsters had to obey was that if any of us wanted to enter the first team dressing-room, then they had to knock on the door and wait until they were told to enter. It did not matter if you had already played in the first team, if you used the reserve dressing-room then you had to knock on the door. If by any chance you walked in without knocking or without being told, then you were told to get out in no uncertain terms."

Having frequently overshadowed the enthralling wing play of the English game's finest in Matthews and Finney, Roger enjoyed pitting his wits against European opposition. In Madrid he was at his international best, keeping a tight reign on their noted French winger Raymond Kopa, who was rarely seen on his flank, as he took to wandering all over the field in an attempt to get more of the ball and to escape Roger's attention.

United were hindered by referee Leo Horn, who seemed to be influenced by the vast majority of the 125,000 crowd in ignoring the gamesmanship of the home side. Fourteen fouls in the opening seven minutes clearly set the mood of the game with the Spaniards obviously aware that United were a side to be reckoned with, trying repeatedly to put them off their game in any way possible.

It was, however, the European Champions who took command of the game after taking the lead in the 60th minute through Rial. Di Stefano made it 2-0 fifteen minutes later, only for Tommy Taylor to pull a goal back eight minutes from time.

With the game poised on a knife-edge, Whelan and Viollet both came close to an equaliser. But with United legs showing signs of tiredness, a Madrid breakaway with five minutes remaining brought a third goal for the home side.

Roger Byrne - Captain of the Busby Babes

Beaten but not downhearted, Roger was quick to offer his thoughts on the game. "Madrid are a good team," he pointed out, "but the bounce of the ball did not go our way. I think, however, we can win the return as we did against Bilbao. We should have had a penalty when Johnny Berry was brought down, but I do not think we played well as a team until we went two goals behind. We certainly have a chance of turning the deficit into success.

"Real Madrid are the best side we have played in the European Cup and I would go as far as to say they are the best side we have faced in any competition."

High praise indeed for the Spaniards, but they had to be pushed to the back of everyone's mind as it was immediately back down to League business two days later with a trip to Luton Town, where two Tommy Taylor goals kept United in pole position with 55 points from 37 games, four in front of Preston North End, who had a game in hand. Tottenham were in third place, six points further adrift.

The Good Friday fixtures produced a local Lancashire derby for United with a short journey to Turf Moor to face Burnley. A Billy Whelan hat-trick, his first goals in thirteen outings, gave United both points in a 3-1 win. Twenty-four hours later, the champagne corks were popping in the United dressing room following a 4-0 victory over Sunderland, which gave them a second successive championship with three games still to play, as their nearest rivals, Preston, had been held to a goalless draw by Blackpool. Whelan had followed his hat-trick with two further goals, Charlton and Taylor notching the others as the first part of the treble was completed in style.

As Roger and his triumphant teammates left the field at full time, the strains of the 'United Calypso' echoed around the ground from the loudspeaker system. In the sanctuary of the dressing room, the captain was already looking to the future as he said: "Although the League title is the least glamorous of the three trophies we are chasing, it is the most arduous. Our ambition now is to win it three years on the run like Huddersfield Town and Arsenal.

"Out on the pitch I did give a little thought as to how Preston North End and Blackpool were faring, but in the end it was really down to ourselves. It will probably take a couple of days to sink in, then it will be time to think about our next match against Madrid. What we must do against them is to reach our top form of the season. Can we win? I am always optimistic."

The stage was set for Old Trafford to host its first European Cup tie as United attempted to overturn the 3-1 deficit against Real Madrid. On the day of the match, the *Daily Herald* carried a large photograph on its back page, of Roger playing bowls at United's Blackpool pre-match headquarters, watched by a pipe-smoking Mark Jones. The accompanying article referred to a famous bowling incident some 369 years previously when Sir Francis Drake enjoyed a similar form of recreation before attempting to repel Spanish invaders, albeit of an entirely different style. However, the odds on success on both occasions were very much against the home side.

Sadly, United could not emulate Drake's triumph over the Spaniards, as they found themselves trailing 5-1 on aggregate after only twenty minutes in what was an ill-tempered affair, the first free kick coming after only 30 seconds. Two goals were pulled back through Tommy Taylor in the 60th minute and Bobby Charlton in the closing minutes, but to no avail, although United did continue to press forward in the hope of reducing the goal difference further.

Shortly after Charlton's goal, Torres, one of the visiting full backs, fell in a heap near his own goalline. The United players were desperate to keep the momentum going and

107

Roger Byrne - Captain of the Busby Babes

Roger was quickly on the scene followed by Edwards, Berry and Charlton, in an attempt to lift the Madrid player off the playing area, much to the annoyance of the Spaniards. A free-for-all almost erupted and when play was eventually resumed, Roger was again involved in the action as inside right Mateos collapsed in a heap following a collision between the two.

The United supporters in the 61,000 crowd, many of whom had gained free admission as, prior to kick-off, police had given away the hundreds of tickets that fans and touts could not sell, continuously booed the Spaniards. They, along with the United players, were severely criticised in the following day's press.

"A squalid show of one-eyed partisanship, a public display of bad manners, they wanted revenge, I was ashamed," proclaimed the headlines preceding George Follows' report in the *Daily Herald*. He went on to blame the crowd for inciting Roger and teammate Duncan Edwards into action they would want to regret.

On Roger, he wrote: "Byrne ended the match on an unhappy note by a blundering foul on Mateos. Nothing can completely excuse this, but the crowd helped them. Seeing victory escaping them, they wanted physical revenge." Not adverse to gamesmanship himself, Roger did not take too kindly to Real's tactics which had been sampled previously in Madrid.

At the end of a game in which the French referee award a total of 51 free kicks (22 against United), the tempers cooled and it was time to reflect on the missed opportunities along with the failure to proceed to greater heights.

"In the two games we played against this team we have learnt every ingenious device ever invented to prevent a team from winning", said Roger," but with Madrid winning 5-3 over the two games, it was I suppose a fair result.

108

Champions of Europe?

"We had too much of the game. We have scored some of our best goals, swinging suddenly from defence to attack. That was also how Madrid's goals came. They are certainly a great side.

"As for the reaction from the crowd throughout the game, they are entitled to their opinion as that is what they pay for."

Roger missed the League fixture at Burnley prior to the Madrid match and the one at Cardiff immediately after it, but returned to the side for the final League outing of the season against West Bromwich Albion to take the plaudits from the supporters as he lifted the League Championship trophy at full-time following the 1-1 draw in front of a disappointing 20,357 crowd.

Receiving the gleaming trophy from Mr Norman Banks of Bolton, a member of the League Management Committee, Roger's voice was drowned by the cheers of the crowd as he said: " I see no reason why we should not win this Cup for the third time in succession next season."

Following the League Championship medal into Roger's trophy cabinet was the *Football Monthly* 'Player Of The Year' award, with the popular magazine carrying the following tribute to the United captain: "At the end of each season, *Football Monthly* selects a 'Player Of The Year'. I have no hesitation, this time, in awarding the honour to Roger Byrne, the Manchester United left back.

"Not only has he played in every England international, but he has led his side to victory in the League championship for the second year running, to the Final of the FA Cup and to the semi-final of the European Cup.

"Though the fame of John Charles, the Wales and Leeds United centre half transferred to Italian club Juventus, and the exploits of Tom Finney, Preston North End's centre forward discovery, have commanded a lot of attention, there can be no denying the wonderful stimulus given by Byrne to both the England and Manchester United teams.

"His cool, calculated work at left back, either when his men are in winning mood or fighting to avoid defeat, have been an inspiration. He rarely plays a poor game.

"Of course Byrne has his detractors who assert that he is too inclined to take risks and prone to lose his balance at times. But one reason why Byrne is undoubtedly the best full back in the country is his confidence in his own ability. What appear to be risks – and would be risks to the ordinary player – are part and parcel of Byrne's immaculate style.

"The square pass back from the by-line to his goalkeeper and the bold dash forward to assist the attack come naturally to Byrne, who started his career as a forward and has complete command of the ball.

"And if Byrne occasionally resents the attention paid to him or his colleagues, it is because he is so wholeheartedly immersed in the game. That he is captain of United proves that these rare moments are insignificant.

"Byrne is still comparatively young at 27 years of age. The longer he plays, the better he will become. He has the brains to make the best use of his great skill.

"Born in Manchester, he has been a United man first and foremost. He has played a conspicuous part in their many successes.

"Byrne is not only a quick thinker but very fast on the run. He has the speed to cope with the fastest of modern wing forwards and the positional sense to limit their activities.

"Most important of all, Byrne always uses the ball to advantage. His well-timed clearances have started many England and United attacks from within their own quarters. With either foot, Byrne places the ball from his full back position, straight to the feet of his forwards. It is a relic of his youthful days when he put across many accurate centres from outside left.

110

Champions of Europe?

"Byrne is busy, too, planning for the future. He is training hard to qualify as a physiotherapist and I have no doubt he will become as skilled in this art as he is on the soccer field."

So it was off to Blackpool for the pre-Cup Final build-up, where Roger had slightly more on his mind than the Wembley date, as just over a month later he was due to marry his fiancée Joy. He also had the niggling ankle injury to fully recover from, which had forced him to miss the two fixtures towards the end of the season.

In the days leading up to the Final, in an interview for 'Picture Post' magazine, Roger shocked the United supporters, and possibly Matt Busby, with his reply to being asked what he would do if offered a move to an overseas club?

Strangely, he answered that: "I would certainly consider it, although I think I am perhaps too old for any such offers to come my way."

Money would obviously have been the prime factor in any contemplated move, as the Spanish and Italian clubs could pay much higher salaries than their British counterparts. It was not, however, the be-all and end-all, as Roger was earning £15 per week plus bonuses with United and his fees from the newspaper articles and England appearances helped to boost this. Joy earned £400 per year as a physiotherapist, while home was a club-owned, three bedroom, semi-detached house in Flixton.

At Blackpool, the United players found it rather difficult to relax and keep the forthcoming Wembley date at the back of their minds, with the demands of the press and television contingent, who seemed to be ever-present, taking up quite a bit of time. The all-white Cup Final strip also received an airing as the players posed for individual and team group photographs.

Despite the many distractions during the build up to

111

the Final, Roger still had time to think of others as Elizabeth Smith recalled. "The Cup Final was, of course, a very special occasion and each player and member of the United staff were allowed to take two guests to the game. Joy was, of course, Roger's main guest and he took my husband as his second. My mother and I were my father's two guests, so this most generous gesture, which we will always remember, enabled my husband to attend the game. Roger also arranged for the Principal of the Salford Royal Hospital School of Physiotherapy to go with the official party, accompanied by her nephew."

"On the Friday we headed south to our Hendon Hall headquarters," Roger was to write in a later article, "while the wives and girlfriends headed to London. It was an early night for all concerned and I am sure that the others went to sleep wondering what tomorrow would bring.

"On the Saturday morning, we had breakfast in bed and our usual lunch of steak, toast and tea before going the few miles to Wembley at around two o'clock. Matt Busby planned as late a departure as possible to try and minimise any nerves.

"The nerves and a tingle of excitement certainly materialised as the twin towers appeared into view and as we drove through the sea of humanity surging up Wembley Way, Duncan Edwards began to sing 'I never felt more like running away', a line from a popular song of the time.

"Once into the south dressing-room of the stadium we soon began our normal pre-match routines and before we knew it we were walking up the tunnel alongside the Aston Villa team and onto the pitch."

As Roger presented his teammates to the Duke of Edinburgh, little did he realise that his hopes of leading United to a coveted League and Cup double would be dealt a stunning blow some ten minutes later.

The game began quietly as the players of both teams

came to grips with the Wembley turf. However, with only six minutes played the eventual destiny of the famous trophy was decided in one goalmouth incident.

Sewell, the Villa left half, lobbed the ball forward to McParland, whose header was comfortably held by Ray Wood in the United goal. Surprisingly, the Villa no 11 followed through on Wood with the Irishman's shoulder catching the goalkeeper's cheekbone.

Wood fell to the ground clutching his face as his teammates hurried to his side. A stretcher was called for and the unfortunate keeper was carried off, with Jackie Blanchflower, on Roger's instructions, pulling on the blood-stained green jersey to take over between the posts. It was a role not unfamiliar to the Irish international, having played for 90 minutes as goalkeeper against Helsingborg in a 5-1 pre-season friendly almost a year earlier.

Blanchflower was certainly immune to any nerves and twice in a matter of minutes pulled off fine saves to keep the scoresheet blank.

With only ten men, Roger had to regroup his defence, but thanks to sterling work from not only himself but also from Bill Foulkes, they managed to safeguard the stand-in goalkeeper from any impeding danger.

Ray Wood reappeared on the touchline five minutes before the interval and took up a position on the wing, where although not of much use, he made it necessary for Villa to employ a man to mark him.

To the surprise of many packed on the Wembley terraces and in homes around the country watching and listening to the events unfold on television and radio, United left the field at half-time on level terms. Indeed, the game remained goalless until the 60th minute when the villain of the afternoon, Peter McParland, eventually beat the heroic Blanchflower with a header from a Smith centre.

Minutes later United were really up against it, as the

same individual put Villa two up with another piece of controversy, shooting past Blanchflower, having moved back from an offside position as Myerscough's shot rebounded off the bar.

Roger, in one of his finest Wembley performances, urged his men on as United never gave up, receiving their reward seven minutes from time when an Edwards corner was headed home by Tommy Taylor.

Wood was quickly returned to his original position, but much as United pressed forward the equaliser failed to materialise as Villa pulled everyone back into defence. Fate had dealt United a cruel blow.

One newspaper reporter, Joe Hulme of *The People*, felt that it was not bad luck which had robbed United of their sought-after double and under the heading of "United Threw It Away", wrote that "they had waited too long before putting Ray Wood back into goal and had they made the move fifteen minutes earlier they would have equalised. When the move was made, the Babes were all over Villa but there was just not enough time to get that second goal.

"Roger Byrne, however, doesn't agree with me. 'I didn't put Wood back in goal earlier because he wasn't fit enough. In fact, he should not have come back at all', he said."

Former United captain Johnny Carey, who had led them to their 1948 Cup success, reflected on the ninety minutes and said: "Struggling under terrific handicaps, Roger Byrne captained his teammates well. He and Jackie Blanchflower were outstanding.

"I hope no one will criticise Roger for not bringing Wood into goal sooner. Although he gallantly returned to the right wing, it was obvious that because of his injury he was, until the closing stages of the game, definitely under the weather."

The outcome of the match was debated long after the final whistle with further criticism, aimed not solely at Roger but at the United defence as a whole, appearing in the Monday edition of the *News Chronicle and Daily Despatch*. This time it surprisingly came from Aston Villa's Peter McParland. The matchwinner made a scathing attack on Roger and his co-defenders, claiming he was "roughed up" following his collision with Ray Wood.

"I was made the target for a personal attack that was obvious retaliation by players who considered I had purposely hit the goalkeeper. It was the worst handling I have ever experienced in football," complained the Villa winger.

McParland continued with the following allegations: "I was struck on the jaw as I went up for a ball in the air, while on another occasion when I leapt to head a ball, an elbow was rammed into my back. Later I was hit in the back of the neck as I fell in a tackle with a United player sprawling across me." The Villa man added that when he suspected a personal attack he moved into the penalty area as often as possible in the hope of winning a penalty.

The controversy of the Final lingered on for some time. The United players, families and friends drowned their sorrows at their after-match banquet in the Savoy Hotel, travelling back to Manchester the following day to a tumultuous welcome. Thousands packed into Albert Square and the roar could not have been louder had Roger carried the Cup itself on the open-topped bus.

Despite their obvious disappointment, there were smiles on the faces of the United players as they met the Lord Mayor of Manchester on the Town Hall steps, where amid the cheers and shouts from the crowd of "never mind 'Rog', you did wonders. You are still all our heroes," the United captain stepped towards the microphone.

There was immediate silence, as he said: "What City can do we can do. They won through two years on the run and won the Cup the second time. I don't see why we can't equal that record. We have lost the double, but we have, I think earned the praises for our wonderful fighting spirit. I am proud of the way the team fought after Ray Wood's injury. It was a knock out blow to us but I am hoping we shall be at Wembley again next year."

Having had time to reflect on the ninety minutes at Wembley, Roger gave his thoughts on the controversial afternoon in the Monday edition of the *Manchester Evening News* and under the heading of "I'm Really Proud Of The Boys Now" he wrote: "Well it's been an adventurous season, and though the English and the European Cup have eluded our grasp for this year at any rate, no Manchester United player is going into mourning. For the simple reason that we have every reason to be extremely proud of our tremendous performances this winter.

"All of us were, of course, hopeful of succeeding at Wembley, but it seems as if fate or whatever you call it had decided otherwise.

"What would have happened if Ray Wood had not been hurt early in the game with Aston Villa is another matter. I think we might now have been reading a very different story. But we were virtually a man short most of the time and that is too stiff a penalty when you are fighting tooth-and-nail in the Cup Final.

"Now, let us look back at the game. In the first place I had hoped to win the toss, because a brisk wind was blowing right down the pitch from goal to goal, but Johnny Dixon beat me to it.

"The opening minutes were very testing for us, revealing quite clearly that Villa's earnest desire was to obtain the confidence of an early goal. The position became even worse when, in the eighth minute, Ray was carried off and we had to switch Jackie Blanchflower into goal, thus disorganising our normal positioning.

"So there we were, struggling almost from the start. Yet

I was glad to note it only served to force all of us to roll up our sleeves still further. I thought we came through that exacting test with honours. In fact, it made me feel justifiably proud when every one of my colleagues strove just that extra bit more to make up for the loss of a player. Nevertheless, we all felt better when, after an absence of half-an-hour, Ray returned, though he took up the unaccustomed outside right position.

"It was a first half of which I think we had every reason to be proud, though naturally as we gathered together in the dressing room with our manager, all of us were terribly disappointed being a man short. When Ray had to stay behind for further treatment we were up against it with a vengeance on taking the field for the second half.

"It might be said that we had two narrow escapes nearing three-quarter time, with Villa already leading by two goals. For McParland had headed against the post and Myerscough had shot wide. But while giving praise to the Irish international winger, I think it should be admitted that we continued to contest every yard and we were in with a good chance right to the last whistle."

Roger, along with teammates Tommy Taylor and Duncan Edwards had to quickly pick themselves up from the Wembley disappointment, as four days later they were back beneath the twin towers, this time in the white of England to face the Republic of Ireland, who included Billy Whelan in their line-up, in a World Cup qualifier. This match was followed by similar outings against Denmark in Copenhagen on May 15th and the return against the Irish in Dublin four days later.

The trio of international fixtures, Roger's 28th, 29th and 30th caps, still did not bring an end to the season as two days after returning from Dublin he was off again, this time with United to fulfil two friendly fixtures against Copenhagen XIs in Denmark.

Roger Byrne - Captain of the Busby Babes

It was rather surprising that Roger actually went on this trip as he was suffering from blistered feet and only offered to play when Albert Scanlon pulled out at the last minute. Wearing an old pair of training shoes, he lined up in his old outside left position, but failed to complete the ninety minutes, being replaced by Dennis Viollet who scored the winner three minutes from the end in a 3-2 victory.

"Byrne on the wing was not a success", proclaimed one of the headlines from a source who obviously was unaware of the player's physical condition. In the second match, Roger was fit enough to complete the whole game, again at outside left, and he helped United to a 4-3 triumph.

At long last Roger's boots could be thrown to the back of the cupboard, although there was still one further date circled on the calendar – Saturday June 5th 1957, his wedding day.

Roger and his best man Jack Pickles, a close friend, arrived at St Mary's Church, Droylsden, in the warm morning sunshine, twenty minutes before to the 11 o'clock service to find a large number of both adults and children eagerly awaiting his arrival. Many wore United colours and clutched cameras, while a hopeful few carried autograph books. Standing on the church steps were Roger's groomsmen E.Barnes, E.Blinkhorn, H.Henfry, N.Cox and former teammate Don Gibson.

By the time Roger and Joy emerged from the church as husband and wife, following the service conducted by the Rev H.W.Hewitt, the awaiting crowd had increased to a few hundred and required a dozen policemen to try and keep things under control.

Even on his wedding day, it was impossible to make a total escape from football, as teammates Ray Wood, Jeff Whitefoot and Dennis Viollet, along with Eric Evans, formed an arch consisting of football boots hanging from poles decorated with red and white ribbons.

118

Champions of Europe?

Following the wedding photographs, it was off to Paddy McGrath's Cromford Club along with their 75 guests for the reception. "Paddy and his wife were always very kind to us," said Joy, "so we decided to have our wedding reception at the club, which was at that time a popular haunt for many of the United players. In late afternoon, Roger and I left the Cromford Club to fly to Jersey for what I thought would be a nice leisurely honeymoon. Little did I know what was in store.

"After arriving at our hotel and unpacking we went down for a pre-dinner drink. I noticed Roger in conversation with a rather familiar looking face at the bar and when recognition did come, it was something of a shock, as I had last seen our fellow guest a few weeks previously at Wembley in the colours of Aston Villa and I can't say I took favourably to him then. His name was Peter McParland. Roger, however, was speaking to him like a long-lost friend. I suppose though that was typical of Roger, who bore no grudges.

"Jean and Jackie Blanchflower were also on honeymoon on the island, having married the previous Saturday and they had met up with a few more professional footballers and arranged a couple of cricket and football matches against local opposition. Roger was, of course, invited to join them and needless to say, did not have to be asked twice.

"To be honest, I did not mind him playing, as his life was spent playing football, cricket and golf. I was quite used to it. We also spent some time during our fortnight's honeymoon watching the tennis at Wimbledon on television."

So, on Sunday June 23rd Roger returned to one of his boyhood passions, cricket, turning out for a Headmaster's XI against a De La Salle XI. Alongside him were four other professional footballers – McPherson and McBride of

119

Roger Byrne - Captain of the Busby Babes

Walsall, Hogg of Leicester City and Roger's Cup Final adversary Peter McParland.

During the afternoon's play Roger showed that he could easily have made the grade as a cricketer, receiving praise in the *Jersey Evening Post* the following day, with their correspondent writing: "Byrne was proving to be an able bowler in addition to being a sound batsman. Along with McPherson he opened the bowling for the visitors and they proved to be faster than their slow run-up implied."

During the first innings, the Headmaster's XI ran up a score of 147 for 9, with Roger making 20 before being out caught. The opposition were all out for 27, Roger taking two wickets for 8 runs, with McParland catching one off Roger's bowling.

His bowling certainly caused the opposition problems, with one opposing batsman having to leave the field injured when one delivery lifted viciously.

Four days later at People's Park, St Hellier, Roger and his footballing collegues from the cricket eleven were joined by a few other holidaying professionals to take part in a charity football match.

Under the guise of the 'England Ramblers', they took on the Jersey Sandhoppers, who were no match for £150,000 worth of Football League talent. The Ramblers' side read – V.McBride (Walsall); P.Goss (Corinthians), R.Hogg (Aston Villa); G.Fincham (Liverpool), A.McPherson (Walsall), D.Edwards (United); A.Finney (Sheff Wed), R.Byrne, P.McParland (Aston Villa), A.Rowley (Leicester City) and D.Hogg (Leicester City).

The United contingent should have numbered one more, but Jackie Blanchflower was unable to play due to a "slight disposition". He did, however, attempt to watch the afternoon's entertainment from the touchline, but spent most of the game under siege by young autograph hunters.

Played with the temperature well into the 80's, both

120

sides were relieved that each half was to be of only 35 minutes duration. By full-time, the Jersey side were even more relieved that the game was twenty minutes less than normal. The 2,000 crowd, however, spread around the ground enjoyed the afternoon's sport and their all-too-rare glimpse of professional players.

The plimsoll-wearing experienced League eleven also enjoyed the light-hearted fun, but did not take it too easy, maintaining the pace throughout despite the heat. Thankfully there were to be no injuries during the seventy minutes play, although three pairs of plimsolls did receive some half-time repair work.

The Ramblers took little time to settle with their deft and speedy passes creating openings for their forwards and it came as no surprise that they took an early lead through McParland.

Not to be upstaged by an Aston Villa player for the second time in recent weeks, Duncan Edwards took command of the game, covering every inch of the weather-beaten pitch and supplying his attack whenever possible. He also had an eye for goal, scoring twice with a couple of searing drives.

During the half-time interval, with the visitors 5-0 in front, Jean Blanchflower and Joy helped to raise around £45 for charity by going round the ground with collecting tins.

The second half continued where the first left off and despite the passing of a much-appreciated ice lolly around the players during play, the Ramblers scored a further six with the home side managing only a consolation effort in reply. Peter McParland finished top scorer with four, while Roger could only claim one from his inside right position.

The *Jersey Evening Post* was once again most complimentary to the United captain with the following: "Manchester United's immaculate left back, Roger Byrne, demonstrated that his forward ability is on a par by also

Roger Byrne - Captain of the Busby Babes

notching an excellent goal." International or friendly fixture, Roger always gave 100% and was a credit to his profession.

FROM TRIUMPH TO TRAGEDY

D espite the somewhat extended season, coupled with the disappointment of failure in two cup competitions, Roger returned to pre-season training refreshed and eager to begin a renewed assault on the FA and European Cups as well as being determined to lead the club to the retention of the League Championship trophy for a third successive season.

Preparations for the 1957-58 season, however, did not run quite as smoothly as normal, despite victories in both the pre-season friendlies played in Germany. The club came in for some strong criticism following an approach from the BBC with a request to make a training film involving the players.

The request was accompanied by an offer from the BBC to pay each player £10 for taking part in the programme, but this was immediately turned down quite firmly as being too small a sum. The media quickly picked up the story and very soon Manchester United were labelled a team of "big heads", much to Roger's annoyance.

Always quick to defend his teammates, Roger immediately sprang onto the defensive. "I can tell you that the team as a whole firmly believe that as professional footballers who depend on the game for their livelihood, it is no crime to 'cash in' on whatever talents that we may possess, or on the successes which have come our way."

He was also given two minutes in front of the television cameras to explain the players' decision.

"If anyone is interested enough to make a film of us for commercial purposes, then they should be prepared to make a reasonable offer," Roger explained as the cameras rolled. "We did not want the money just for ourselves. In fact we had agreed that if the £10 offer had been stepped up, the cash would have gone to the Footballers' Benevolent Fund. So please lay off that 'United too big for their boots' tag".

The title defence began in fine form with five wins and a draw in the opening six fixtures, scoring twenty-two goals in the process and conceding only five. This gave United a two-point lead at the top, ahead of Nottingham Forest.

Roger and Joy quickly settled down to married life, their spare time taken up with numerous jobs around the house. Roger, however, readily admitted that he was "really quite useless domestic-wise" and was rather relieved that the building of a garage on the side of the house gave him a little less gardening to do!

Joy found no problems adjusting to life as a footballers wife, with her own work commitments keeping her busy when Roger was away. "If United played in the South of England they usually travelled the day before, staying overnight in a hotel," recalled Joy, " I would normally meet Roger off the train on the Saturday night, either at Stockport or Manchester's London Road station.

"For home fixtures, the team would meet for a pre-

124

match lunch at Davyhulme Golf Club. I would go to most of the home games and wait for Roger in the car afterwards. There was no players' lounge or anything like that in those days and it was quite a few years before I actually saw the likes of the directors' lounge."

Revenge for the FA Cup Final defeat came on October 22nd when Aston Villa were beaten 4-0 at Old Trafford in the Charity Shield. There was quite a bit of animosity surrounding the fixture, but this was defused prior to the kick-off when Roger relinquished his captain's role to allow Ray Wood to lead out United alongside Villa's Peter McParland.

By now, United had slipped in the title chase, down to fifth place on 17 points, six behind leaders Wolves, although they did have a game in hand over the Midlands side. On the European front, Shamrock Rovers had been relatively easily disposed of 9-2 on aggregate in the opening round.

The short journey to Preston on November 9th caused Roger considerable problems as he complained to Matt Busby of pain from a boil under his left arm. It was therefore decided to stop the team bus and telephone back to Manchester for Ian Greaves to come and join the party as a precaution, with Roger to be given a fitness test upon arriving at Deepdale.

The test was subsequently passed and the United captain played his part in the 1-1 draw, recovering sufficiently to play his 250th League and Cup match the following Saturday, against Sheffield Wednesday at Old Trafford.

Results continued to vary from week to week, with the defence leaking more goals than normal – eight in three games as November ran into December. This prompted Matt Busby into making a move into the transfer market and he bolstered the United rearguard with the signing of Northern Ireland international goalkeeper Harry Gregg from

Roger Byrne - Captain of the Busby Babes

Doncaster Rovers for a fee of £23,500.

"I already knew many of the United players from international fixtures," said Harry, "so it didn't take me long to settle. After I signed for the club I actually lived with Roger and Joy for a while and found them a really lovely couple."

Joy was quick to return the compliment and went on to recall an amusing incident which occurred during Harry's time in the Byrne household. "We used to have a dog," explained Joy, "and it took quite a liking to him. One morning, however, it got a little more excited than usual in Harry's room as it woke him up, leaving a damp patch on the bedroom floor.

"Harry noticed this wet area on the carpet when he got up and immediately thought he had spilled something the night before and quickly tried to dry it up, much to both mine and Roger's amusement."

With Harry Gregg in goal, Roger and his defensive colleagues had to adjust their tactics slightly, as the big Irishman explained. "Ray Wood was more of a goalline keeper than I was. In my opinion, the penalty box was my domain and if the ball came into it, I went for it. In my first match against Leicester City, Duncan Edwards was sent sprawling as he did not get out of the way quick enough when I came out for a cross. Roger and the others soon got the idea of how I played and an understanding was quickly reached.

"I found Roger an exceptional person both on and off the pitch. He did not need an armband or anything to show that he was captain. It was obvious by the way he performed that he was. He had the total respect of all the players."

The football-loving youngsters of the 1950's eagerly looked forward to Christmas and the numerous annuals that appeared at this time of year. One of the most popular

126

of these publications was the *FA Book For Boys* and within its pages, youngsters were offered the opportunity of interviewing one of the top players of the day. Readers were invited to send in a list of questions to ask a player of a certain position and the writer of the best questions would meet the player and appear in the annual.

In the 1957 edition, Trevor Sargeant from Lewisham became the envy of his friends when his questions for a full back were considered the best and he was invited to Arsenal's Highbury Stadium to come face-to-face with the full back who topped the poll of who the readers wanted to interview – Roger Byrne.

In the 1950's there was not the same media coverage as today and the schoolboy's questioning of Roger revealed the United captain's thoughts and defensive secrets, which in today's high-profile environment would be well documented.

"The art of playing full back is to be able to make the winger go where you want him to," Roger replied to an early question. "It is fatal to rush into a tackle and you should bide your time. By backing away from the winger, you can place yourself between him and the goal, so that he can do the least harm."

"What about the winger who keeps moving away from you?" enquired the youngster. "Is a sliding tackle best?" "Only as a last resort," the master replied, "as it leaves you in an awkward position if the tackle goes wrong. A winger has less chance if you cut down the room he has to manoeuvre in."

When asked about a winger who wanders all over the place, Roger admitted that they caused problems and an understanding had to be made with your teammate playing immediately in front of you at wing half.

Roger and his young admirer practised a few moves on the Highbury pitch before proceeding with further advice. "Make every pass count," advised Roger, before going on to persuade Trevor against attempting to play the offside trap. The youngster was also advised against taking his opponent for granted. "He might not seem up to much," he was told, "but never forget about him. You can't afford to relax for an instant. It's often the indifferent players, the ones we tend to neglect, who score the surprise goals."

Out on the Arsenal pitch, Roger demonstrated to the schoolboy the strength of his passing skills. Short passes to an imaginary half back or a long clearance up the wing were both carried out with supreme accuracy, along with the instructions to "make every pass count".

Needless to say, it was a thrilling experience for the schoolboy to not only ask the United captain questions about the game, but to also enjoy kicking the ball about on the famous Highbury pitch with one of the big names in British football.

With Harry Gregg's arrival, results improved, although United still trailed behind leaders Wolves by eight points at the turn of the year. The FA Cup gave the team the opportunity to forget the fight to retain their Championship crown and attempt to make a return journey to Wembley. The third-round draw paired United with Third Division Workington Town and the Cumbrian side were to prove no pushovers.

Catching United on the hop, they opened the scoring after only five minutes through Colbridge and for most of the first half the visitors continued to struggle against their lesser opponents. After the interval, United began to find their feet, equalising in the 54th minute through Dennis Viollet. This broke the Cumbrians' resistance and urged on by Roger, "the coolest man on the pitch", going by one report, they were 3-2 in front eight minutes later, Viollet the hat-trick hero.

January 14th brought Red Star Belgrade to Manchester for the first leg of the European Cup quarter-final tie, with the thick mist which enveloped the ground making it difficult for many to see most of the action. Those who could distinguish the players enjoyed a memorable encounter.

Harry Gregg's habit of rushing from his goalline was not admired by everyone and as a result of one such dangerous excursion, United found themselves a goal behind, with Tasic lobbing the ball over his head from some thirty yards out to give Red Star the lead after thirty-five minutes.

As the second half got under way, the mist began to lift, as did United's determination. Inspired by Duncan Edwards, who created the opening for Charlton to equalise, United ignored the body-checking, elbowing and shirt-pulling of the Yugoslavs. With only nine minutes remaining, a rare Eddie Colman goal gave them a 2-1 lead. Many felt that this slender advantage would not be enough to take United into the semi- finals a fortnight later.

Four days later, the Bolton bogey was exorcised, at least for the time being, as a 7-2 win stretched the unbeaten run to six games without defeat, while Ipswich Town succumbed to a 2-0 defeat in the fourth round of the FA Cup.

Before Matt Busby could prepare his team for the return leg against Red Star Belgrade, there was an important League fixture against Arsenal, at Highbury, to fulfil. Too many drawn games had left United still six points behind leaders Wolves, but there was still time to close the gap, with the Molineux men due in Manchester seven days later.

Arsenal, although in mid-table, were always formidable opposition and the 63,578 spectators inside the North London ground that afternoon enjoyed a classic encounter.

United's pre-match preparations were unsettled when 82-year-old club director George Whittaker was found dead in his London hotel room on the morning of the match. Mr

Roger Byrne - Captain of the Busby Babes

Whittaker had been a director for 22 years. Black armbands were worn as a mark of respect and stood out on the sleeves of United's white shirts as Roger led an unchanged team for the sixth successive fixture onto the soft Highbury turf.

In no time at all, play was flowing from end to end with the home side soon on the defensive with Tommy Taylor failing to make the most of a Foulkes free kick following a foul by Evans on Morgans, sending his header off target. Minutes later, it was Morgans, who had still to open his scoring account, scorning an ideal opportunity with the Arsenal defence again in disarray. Gregg thwarted Herd, who created an opening with Bloomfield, and the goalkeeper's clearance reached Scanlon, who centred across the face of the Gunners' goal, where the waiting Morgans lofted the ball over the bar.

Both goalkeepers had to be alert in those opening exchanges and were called into further action with Gregg saving at the feet of Vic Groves, while Kelsey showed sharp reactions as he made a superb save from a fine Tommy Taylor effort. It was the home custodian, however, who was the first to retrieve the ball from the back of the net as United opened the scoring in the tenth minute.

Kenny Morgans, having already caused the Arsenal defence considerable trouble down the right, moved inside and squared the ball into the path of the oncoming Edwards. Although some twenty-five yards from goal, mere inches for the Dudley giant, he struck the ball firmly and though Kelsey managed to get his fingers to it, the power of the shot carried it into the back of the net.

Unperturbed, Arsenal continued to look for an opening and a long ball out of defence saw United's rearguard looking for an offside which failed to materialise, leaving centre forward Herd chasing the ball. Fortunately for United, Gregg was alert to the impending danger, dashing from his goal area to kick clear.

130

United slowly began to monopolise the game, with an Edwards-Taylor move ending with the latter's shot being saved by Kelsey. An Edwards free kick passed just wide of the goal with the goalkeeper beaten, while a Scanlon cross caused panic in the goalmouth before being scrambled clear. Arsenal made brief excursions into the United area and both Roger and Harry Gregg were called upon to make interceptions and saves to prevent the home side from drawing level.

With thirty-four minutes played, United increased their lead, thanks mainly to outside left Scanlon. Collecting Gregg's clearance just inside his own half, his seventy-yard run down the wing left Charlton (the Arsenal full back) standing, while his pin-point cross found Bobby Charlton, who shot past Kelsey before the keeper could move.

Arsenal, to their credit, continued in their attempts to salvage something from a game which was slowly slipping away from them even although it was not yet half-time. For a split second, their players and supporters thought they had indeed pulled a goal back through Tapscott, just before the interval, but a linesman's raised flag ended the premature celebrations.

Play quickly moved to the opposite end of the pitch and Charlton's shot beat Kelsey, but was diverted over the bar by full back Evans. Loud claims for handball and a penalty came from the United players, but following consultation with his linesman, referee Pullin awarded only a corner.

As the minutes ticked away towards the end of the first half, Kelsey once again prevented United from scoring with a superb save from a Viollet header. The Welsh international, however, failed to stop United going 3-0 up seconds before the break, when Tommy Taylor pushed the ball past the keeper at the second attempt following a neat pass from Morgans. Much to Arsenal's relief, the whistle blew for half- time and the applause for United's performance echoed around the ground as both teams left the field for a well-deserved break.

During the interval, Arsenal decided to switch wingers Groves and Tapsott, so Roger found himself up against a different opponent as the second half got underway. Manager Jack Grayston's decision soon proved beneficial as thirteen minutes into the half they pulled a goal back. Their captain, Dave Bowen, surged forward and passed to centre forward David Herd who beat Gregg without much of a problem. This seemed to alter the Gunners' attitude to the game with their play taking on a new form of determination, giving Roger and his fellow defenders much more to think about. Two minutes later, Gregg had conceded two further goals as the atmosphere reached fever pitch with Arsenal drawing level.

First, a cross from the left found Bloomfield ideally situated to guide the ball past Gregg, and with United reeling, the same player propelled the ball past Gregg a second time, via an upright. Arsenal 3, United 3!

The crowd went delirious as the outcome of the match looked to have changed completely. Many lesser clubs would have folded completely, allowing Arsenal to complete their transformation by going on to score again and take both points in an epic afternoon's entertainment.

This, however, was Manchester United and no ordinary team. Inspired by the half back partnership of Edwards and Colman and the skill of Scanlon wide on the left, with Roger organising everything from the back, United clawed their way back into the game as the crowd swayed with every movement out on the muddied pitch.

Following a desperate clearance, Roger required treatment and as he eased himself back into the fray United took the lead. Albert Scanlon drifted past the hapless

Charlton and crossed into the Arsenal goalmouth where Viollet headed firmly past Kelsey.

Arsenal attempted to breach the United defence with numerous long balls and Gregg had to be alert to stop Groves on one occasion when an opening was created. The keeper's clearance swung play to the opposite end of the Highbury pitch where Morgans beat an oncoming defender before passing to Taylor in a wide position. The United centre forward rounded Evans and from an acute angle fired the ball past Kelsey, whose touch helped it into the net. Seventy-two minutes played, Arsenal 3, United 5.

Five minutes later, the game was once again thrust wide open as Arsenal again pulled a goal back through Tapscott, who collected Herd's pass before beating Gregg with a fine effort.

In the remaining minutes, the home crowd shouted themselves hoarse in an attempt to encourage their heroes into snatching a draw, but United held on to their 5-4 advantage and no one could deny them their victory in a pulsating afternoon's entertainment. Such was the display from both teams that the applause at full time was as loud and prolonged as had greeted any of the nine goals.

The players, like the supporters, realised that they had been part of a footballing spectacle, were quick to shake hands with their opposite numbers, a few leaving the field with arms around one another.

Roger limped out of Highbury and headed back to Manchester, being considered doubtful for Wednesday's match in Yugoslavia against Red Star in the second leg of the European Cup quarter-final tie. The thigh injury required intensive heat treatment at Old Trafford on the Monday night and his chances of playing in the important European match were far from certain. So much so, that reserve team full back Geoff Bent was called into the party to travel to the Yugoslavian capital.

Roger was Matt Busby's only worry as the team settled

into their Belgrade hotel and trainer Tom Curry set about making an old-fashioned poultice to slap onto the badly bruised left thigh. A spell under a sun lamp and a visit to the local hospital followed, before a vigorous workout on the slush-covered Red Star pitch, after which Roger gave his much relieved manager the thumbs up allowing Matt Busby to field the same eleven players who had played three games in a row without defeat.

The doubts of United's 2-1 lead being enough to see them through to the semi-finals disappeared slightly after only ninety seconds when centre half Spajic mis-hit a clearance which rebounded off Taylor to Dennis Viollet, who had little problem in beating Beara in the Red Star goal.

Morgans and Edwards both received knocks as the Yugoslavians became frustrated, cheered on by a fiercely partisan crowd which was quickly silenced by two further United goals in the twenty-ninth and thirty-second minutes from Bobby Charlton, who had seen an earlier effort ruled out for offside.

With a 5-1 aggregate lead, the game looked over but referee Kainer and the Yugoslavians seemed to have other ideas as a dramatic fightback developed in the second half.

Two minutes after the restart, Kostic fired home a twenty-yard shot which was followed by a hotly disputed penalty from Tasic. Red Star pressed forward and United realised that they were up against twelve men, with the referee giving everything to the home side. Gregg took a knock and Roger was spoken to by the referee for time-wasting as United battled to maintain their lead.

With the minutes ticking away, Red Star concluded a creditable fight back with an equaliser, as Kostic's shot hit Viollet and squirmed over Gregg's outstretched arms and into the net. Fortunately there was no time left for any further dramatic developments as the referee's whistle signalled the

The Babes are champions again

Double Vision: Roger wearing his 1957 FA Cup Final shirt. Victory would make United the first double winners in the 20th Century

Roger and Villa opposite number Johnny Dixon battle it out with
pepper pots prior to the 1957 FA Cup Final

But the game doesn't go well for the Reds
Aston Villa 2 United 1

Roger and Joy relax in their Flixton home

United pose before heading off on a
1957-58 pre-season tour of Germany

Roger leads
United out at
Highbury,
the Babes'
last domestic
fixture

The post-match dinner in Belgrade: Roger Byrne signs an autograph for a fan while Matt Busby looks on - there are no other players in this photograph.

THE FOOTBALL LEAGUE LIMITED

List of Professional Players of the MANCHESTER UNITED Club during the period 1st JANUARY, 1957, to 31st DECEMBER, 1957, and their gross emoluments during that period.

For League Office Use		SURNAME (Alphabetical Order)	CHRISTIAN NAMES (In full)		Period of Employment during 1957 From To		Wages, including Bonus, Talent Money, etc.			Benefit and/or Accrued Share of Benefit paid during 1957			For League Office Use
4983	1	BARRETT	GEORGE THOMAS	√	1.1.57	27.7.57	208	12	6	500	0	0	Plymouth
4387	2	BENT	GEOFFREY	√	1.1.57	31.12.1957.	778	12	0				
197	3	BERRY	JOHN	√	"	"	1169	9	0				NR I/K1
	4	BESWICK	IVAN	"	29.6.57		154	5	0				
3670	5	BLANCHFLOWER	JOHN	√	"	31.12.1957.	1042	13	7				NE.
	6	BRATT	HAROLD	√	9.11.57	"	90	10	0				
6624	7	BRENNAN	SEAMUS	√	1.1.57	"	359	17	6				
2993	8	BYRNE	ROGER WILLIAM	√	"	"	1188	17	2				
				√	"		550	2	6				

Football League wage sheets from 1957 (above) and 1958 (below)

		Bradley	Warren	√	10.11.1958.	31.12.1958.	145	0	0	√			NE.
7627		Bratt	Harold	√	1.1.58	"	601	0	0				
662+		Brennan	Seamus Anthony	√	"	"	892	0	0				
		Byrne (deceased)	Roger William		"	6.2.58	193	0	0				NR I/K9
7166		Carolan	Joseph	√	"	31.12.1958.	805	15	0				
6130		Charlton	Robert	√	"	"	1014	0	0				
5606		Clayton	Gordon	√	"	"	751	10	0				
		Colman (deceased)	Edward		"	6.2.58	193	0	0				NR I/K9
4459		Cope	Ronald	√	"	31.12.1958.	1129	0	0				Aston v Chelsea
665		Crowther	Stanley	√	19.2.58	16.12.1958.	963	0	0				
7700		Dawson	Alexander Downie	√	1.1.58.	31.12.1958.	914	5	0				
		Edwards (deceased)	Duncan		"	6.2.58.	227	0	0				NR I/K9

Roger's funeral at St. Michael's, Flixton

The Babes line-up during their last season

ght: Roger's dedication in the United Museum
Below: As Roger and the rest of the team are
remembered in Newton Heath

ROGER BYRNE
CLOSE

MILLWRIGHT STREET
LEADING TO
TOMMY TAYLOR CLOSE
EDDIE COLMAN CLOSE
BILLY WHELAN WALK
GEOFF BENT WALK
ROGER BYRNE CLOSE
DAVID PEGG WALK

Roger William Byrne
1929 - 1958

Wedding photographs courtesy of Mrs Joy Worth.
All other photographs courtesy of Iain McCartney's private collection.
United team cards courtesy of John Fitzhugh.

end of the game. United were into the semi-finals of the European Cup for the second successive season.

It was a very relieved Roger Byrne at full time and in the after-match interviews he reflected that: "It had been a difficult game to play in, as the referee's performance had forced us to stop tackling due to good tackles being penalised with free kicks. We were not so worried when we were winning, but after that penalty we became afraid lest a tackle would mean a free kick in the danger zone."

He added: "Football is a funny game isn't it? I thought we were going to walk it after taking a three-goal lead, but it just shows you that you cannot give these continental sides an inch. Once they get a goal they play like demons. Never mind, we are through to the semi-finals."

Despite the tense and some times physical ninety minutes, the management and players of both sides relaxed and enjoyed the after-match banquet, so much so that as the official get-together drew to an end, Roger approached Matt Busby to ask if the lads could go elsewhere for a few drinks and stay out a bit later. "Half an hour," replied the boss, which quickly brought numerous protests resulting in a further half hour being agreed.

Most of the players, including Roger, made their way to the British Embassy Staff Club, where drinking and dancing saw the one o'clock Busby curfew quickly come around. A BEA rep and his wife drove Roger and Mark Jones back to the team hotel, but with the adrenaline still in full flow, a quick exit was made from the rear of the hotel. They climbed back into the BEA rep's car and along with a member of the British Embassy staff they were taken to a Canadian couple's home for some further liquid refreshment. It was 3.00am when Roger and his centre half finally returned to their hotel, managing only a few hours' sleep before it was time for the journey back to Manchester.

By the time the United party arrived at Belgrade's

Roger Byrne - Captain of the Busby Babes

Zemun Airport the following morning, the sore heads from the night before had quickly cleared, thanks to cups of strong coffee and the cold early-morning air. The Yugoslavian newspapers were quickly glanced over as there was little time to waste before being called to the door of the departure lounge by a Yugoslavian official. He handed out the passports to the forty-four passengers who then filed onto the awaiting Elizabethan AS57 airliner G-ALZU.

No sooner was the plane airborne than the card schools were in full flow, with Jackie Blanchflower, Dennis Viollet, Liam Whelan, Ray Wood and Roger quickly engrossed in their hands.

The blue sky and sunshine of Belgrade was soon transformed into a dull grey, not helped by the falling snow, while the ground was covered in a few inches of snow and slush as the plane touched down at Munich's Riem Airport for a forty minute scheduled re-fuelling stop.

Although only a short walk from the aeroplane to the airport lounge, everyone felt the bitter cold wind upon leaving the plane and quickly made their way to the warmth of the terminal. A chill, however, even filled the lounge as latecomer Roger Byrne held the door open for a bit longer than was necessary, only to be met with some friendly abuse from his teammates. Dressed immaculately as always, in his England blazer, he slowly closed the door and joined the rest of the team for some warm refreshments.

The call soon came to return to the re-fuelled aeroplane, whose wheel tracks of some forty-seven minutes previously were now almost invisible due to the continuously falling snow. Once aboard, there was little point in Roger and his card-playing chums in dealing another hand, as lunch was due to be served following take-off. Everyone quickly settled into their seats and the plane moved off down the runway. But, to everyone's surprise, it came to a sudden halt after travelling only 450 yards.

From Triumph to Tragedy

Minutes later, the Elizabethan was again moving down the runway on a second attempt to take off, but in the cockpit it was noticed that the port side engine was fluctuating badly. The proposed take-off was abandoned on Captain Thain's orders, but it was a further twenty minutes before passengers were allowed to unfasten their seatbelts and once again disembark as the pilots and crew checked out the problem.

With a tough League fixture against Championship challengers Wolverhampton Wanderers at Old Trafford on Saturday, Matt Busby was keen to get his team home, while the journalists on board wanted to be back in Manchester for the Press Ball that evening.

"All aboard," came the call, before anyone could get settled into the warm surroundings. Back to the dismal looking plane trouped the disgruntled passengers for a third attempt at take-off.

Seatbelts fastened, the aeroplane began to move off slowly down the slushy runway, picking up speed with every yard covered. Within the cabin there was an eerie silence, everyone deep in their own thoughts. Bill Foulkes recalled his as the plane continued to pick up speed with the buildings flashing past the small windows.

"I remember sitting in the plane facing Albert Scanlon," said Bill. "David Pegg had gone up to the back of the plane where he thought it was safer and Eddie Colman had also been told to sit up there out of the way, as he was always carrying-on and being a nuisance. On the opposite side, there was a six-seater table where Roger sat along with Jackie, Ray, Dennis and Billy Whelan. Billy, a devout Roman Catholic muttered something I didn't understand at the time and Roger also said something, which again I couldn't really make out as the noise inside the plane grew louder."

Roger had by now pushed himself deep into his seat, while others gripped tighter to their armrests as the end of

137

the runway flashed past.

Suddenly, the sound of the engines was drowned by an ear-splitting crash as the aeroplane shook violently, spinning off the runway, crashing through the perimeter fence and into a nearby house. Everything was plunged into darkness before the crunch of the breaking fuselage echoed eerily through the cabin.

It was 15.04. Silence enveloped the scene, the final whistle had blown for many on board.

The impact of the crash threw many of the passengers through the broken fuselage and onto the slush and snow which covered the ground around the perimeter of the runway. Roger was one of those, lying still strapped to his seat some thirty yards from the wreckage. Alongside was Matt Busby. One dead, the other barely alive.

Back in Manchester, supporters were still talking about the victory over Red Star, while eagerly anticipating Saturday's top of the table clash with Wolves. Early editions of the *Evening News* and the *Evening Chronicle* carried reports of the Red Star cup-tie and injury updates, while one edition of the *Evening Chronicle* contained the following 'Stop Press' item from their correspondent Alf Clarke under the heading "United Held Up In Germany"– "The triumphant Manchester United footballers, on the way back from Belgrade to Manchester, are held up in Munich by engine trouble and they may not be able to get away until tomorrow.

"United, who drew 3-3 with Red Star Belgrade and so qualified for the European Cup semi-finals, broke their journey at Munich where they had lunch.

"They were due into Ringway this evening, but their plane developed engine trouble and it is doubtful if they will get away today as it is snowing very heavily."

As the minutes ticked past, a much different story began to crackle over the telephone wires with a *Manchester*

From Triumph to Tragedy

Evening News 'Stop Press' displaying the bold headline "United Plane Crashes". Underneath came the grim news: "BEA Elizabethan carrying Manchester United team crashed on take off at Munich airport today.

"Plane crashed 60 feet and is totally wrecked. BEA spokesman said : 'Understood 10 to 15 survivors out of 40 people on board. This is not definitely confirmed.'

"Party included 19 United players, four officials including manager Matt Busby and sports reporters. Tom Jackson of the *Manchester Evening News* is on the plane."

An early newsflash on television and radio told a similar story: "A report from Germany says that the plane, an Elizabethan, carrying Manchester United football team, officials and journalists crashed on take-off at Munich. We will bring you more news later." For those watching or listening, their concentration on the afternoon's entertainment and whatever else they were occupied with suddenly came to an abrupt end.

In Manchester, and indeed throughout Britain, word quickly spread. From home to home, shop to shop, office to factory, with the remainder of the afternoon's production virtually halted. Children, who usually strolled home from school at a leisurely pace, ran, many with tears streaming down the cheeks, hoping that the snatches of conversations that they had heard regarding their red-shirted heroes were no more than a cruel rumour. As factory hooters blew and shops closed, there were frantic dashes to the nearest news vendor for the latest edition of the evening newspapers.

At home in Flixton, a radio news bulletin took Joy Byrne by surprise. "I first heard of the crash around 4.30pm from a radio newsflash," she said, "and it certainly came as a massive shock. I had expected Roger back home by early evening, as he had to go to the ground first to pick up his car, which had been left there by the garage following a service.

Roger Byrne - Captain of the Busby Babes

"The whole of that evening was spent waiting for further news, with the time passing so slowly. Numerous relations and friends congregated at our home, including Roger's parents. We simply sat around watching television and listening to radio news programmes for most of the time. Each summary brought further pieces of information including names of survivors.

"Around midnight I received the telephone call with the news I had been dreading all evening. Roger was dead."

As the story of the tragic events in Germany unfolded, newspaper offices, not only in Manchester but also around the country, became hives of activity with the evening editions becoming somewhat dated, as no sooner was it off the press than further news was wired through.

The headlines in the *Manchester Evening Chronicle* went from "United Held Up In Germany" in their 'Last Extra' edition to "United Air Disaster – 28 Killed" in its 'Late Night Final', only to bring out another edition with a further update of "United Air Disaster – 30 Killed".

The *Manchester Evening News* moved along similar lines, while all around the country the evening editions told similar stories. In the *Birmingham Evening Dispatch* the headline read "Manchester United Plane Crash – 28 Dead", while in the *Ipswich Evening Star* the news was "Manchester United Team In Crashed BEA Liner, 10-15 Passengers Safe".

In a short period of time, the victory placards of "United in European semis" on the news vendors' boards were replaced with "United Disaster".

Crowds soon began gathering outside Old Trafford, hoping for more news than what they had already heard through the media, but there was little more that the United office staff could add. The League Championship flag flying at half mast above the silent stadium said more than any words could.

140

From Triumph to Tragedy

The 6pm edition of the *Manchester Evening Chronicle* carried a 'Stop Press', which brought news of the United captain and renewed hope to those near to him and to those who appreciated his skills on the football field. "Roger Byrne is among saved", it began and continued, " Byrne strove to make himself one of the death defying heroes of the grim drama as fires flared.

"Rescue workers red-eyed from smoke told of courage of Roger Byrne. They said he crawled from the wreckage, his clothes slashed.

"His hand fell on a fire extinguisher thrown clear in the melee of twisted steel. He turned it on small fires already leaping from the wreckage as passengers moaned beneath the tangled metalwork.

"He beat back the flames and then hauled people clear, not caring for the danger as the plane's fuel tanks spilled fuel across yards of ground.

"This story was told from Munich to BEA in London who said: 'Here is the story of a brave man'."

Sadly, although the facts of the heroic deeds were true, the identity of the hero was mistaken for some unknown reason. It was goalkeeper Harry Gregg who had displayed such supreme courage, not his defensive colleague Roger Byrne, who lay silently in the slush near to many of his teammates and friends.

By the following morning, the distressing details of the disaster were on the front page of every newspaper in the country. Not only Manchester, but the whole country was in mourning as the roll call of those talented individuals who had lost their lives was now complete – Liam Whelan, the quiet playmaking Irishman from Dublin. Mark Jones, the well-built and strong-tackling centre half from Barnsley. David Pegg, the skilful outside left who had still to reach his full potential, Eddie Colman, the Salford lad with the deceptive body swerve, Tommy Taylor, England's centre

141

forward, Geoff Bent, the reserve team full back and their captain Roger Byrne.

Club secretary Walter Crickmer, trainer Tom Curry and coach Bert Whalley were also dead, along with eight journalists and three others, while manager Matt Busby and Duncan Edwards were both very seriously ill. Sadly the latter's name was added to those of his teammates who had lost their lives, as the Dudley giant lost his brave fight for life some fifteen days later.

It was kick-off time on the afternoon of Monday February 10th, but the venue was Munich airport, not one of the numerous stadiums around the world graced by Matt Busby's 'Babes'. The snow of four days previously had almost disappeared, but wreckage of the Elizabethan still littered one end of the runway.

Around 150 policemen stood in silent rows behind the official mourners holding countless wreaths which were carried fifty yards to a waiting plane. They were then passed to the chief German BEA officer to carry inside, where the 21 coffins of pale elm had lain since dawn. There were no onlookers, no music, nothing.

Amongst the wreaths were pink camellia from the Munich police, red and white carnations from BEA, two trolley loads of mimosa and white roses from the German Ministry of Transport. There were simple bunches of lillies from journalists, while the last to pass through the door was a bouquet of red and white carnations with the inscription: "The Busby Babes, their biographers and those who died with them," from Jean Busby, the survivors' wives and friends.

The 'Babes' were going home.

At 10.08pm, out of a black Manchester sky, a BEA Viscount freighter, Sir John Madeville, slowly descended towards the runway as the League Championship flag hung limply at half mast in the damp air above the terminal building at Ringway airport. The drone of the aircraft's engine was the only noise.

Standing silently, with their heads bowed, were the Lord Mayor of Manchester, Alderman Leslie Lever, along with United directors Harold Hardman, William Petherbridge and Louis Edwards. Moments after coming to a halt, the doors of the plane opened and 58 wreaths of red carnations and white tulips were carried out, followed by Roger's coffin and those of 16 others. The four others had been removed during a brief stop at London airport.

Although the homecoming was now running some two hours late, the streets between the airport and Old Trafford were still lined with people and cars. Out into Ringway Road the cortege moved, along into Princess Parkway where a double-decker bus was abandoned by passengers and crew alike. Oncoming traffic came to a standstill as a city paid tribute to its favourite sons.

The falling rain did nothing to lessen the numbers who lined the streets, many kneeling in silent prayer, as each hearse slowly passed. Women and children were prominent among the crowd, many wearing red and white scarves and rosettes and faces damp with a mixture of tears and rain, remembering their Saturday heroes.

Into Seymour Grove, where the crowds began to thicken, most having stood for hours, with mounted police now required to keep control. The lads were almost home.

Turning into Warwick Road, it was now after midnight and the seventeen-mile journey was almost at an end. Around the Old Trafford forecourt police struggled to control the vast number of people who at times threatened to break through the cordon. One by one the hearses drew up alongside the main entrance to the ground, off-loading their coffins to lie in the gymnasium beneath the main stand yards from the pitch they had once graced, as the crowds silently moved forward for a better view.

143

Roger Byrne - Captain of the Busby Babes

The large wooden doors closed as the last hearse drove off. Slowly the crowds unwillingly dispersed homewards with their memories of the lads in red shirts transfixed in their minds.

Tributes to those who died flowed thick and fast, with Roger remembered fondly by friend and foe alike. Stanley Matthews, one of the many wingers who failed to gain the upper hand when up against Roger, said: "Football will go on at Old Trafford and Manchester United will rise again, but it will never be the same for visiting teams. We will miss those players who became our friends the enemy, those stars who promised to make United the greatest team of all-time.

"There was Roger Byrne, captain and left back who opposed me many times in the League and played behind me in international games. Very fast and brilliant in recovery, he was always a difficult man to beat.

"As a captain he was making the grade. Given a few years to gain stature and maturity, he might have become one of our greatest captains. He was certainly in line to lead England in the near future.

"He was also a quick thinker. I remember some years ago we were playing Switzerland and Roger beat his man way back in his own corner of the field. He could have blazed the ball upfield, but he stopped to look over the situation. He saw me standing unmarked on the wing and over came a long high ball, perfectly placed to my foot. A flick from me to Jimmy Mullen, a powerful, bullet-like shot and we were another goal up.

"That was Roger Byrne...full of confidence, almost cheeky in his approach to the game and a man destined to line up with the all-time greats of football."

From A.M.Bodoano MCSP, Principal of the Salford Hospital Management Committee School of Physiotherapy came the following: "Always renown for his prowess as a footballer but to us in the School of Physiotherapy he will be remembered for his fine character and loving personality.

From Triumph to Tragedy

"He was a part-time student in training and had special permission from the Chartered Society of Physiotherapy to undertake his training part-time over a period of six years instead of the usual three full-time.

"He was well-liked and popular with the staff and students and was also determined to make a success of his training. At no time did he preside in the fact that he was something of a national hero and he was completely without conceit and self-satisfaction. He took his place with the other students and worked industriously and steadily. As a result, he was successful in passing the preliminary examination of the Chartered Society and was preparing to take the intermediate examination this year.

"We feel that we personally have lost a great friend and the physiotherapy profession have lost an excellent student."

His good friend and fellow sportsman Eric Evans paid his tribute to Roger in the *Ashton Reporter* with the following: "It is a great blow to me to hear of the tragic death of my friends Bert Whalley and Roger Byrne, whom I have been closely associated with during the past year.

"It has been said that Roger has a similar temperament to my own, but I can say this, he was a most unassuming man despite his success. He always remembered his pals and his school days and the little things in life, which are often overlooked.

"Before any big match, Roger and I always discussed each other's problems and worries, and helped each other. We always ran around the ground together as well, before any big game and I considered it a bad omen if we missed this little ritual.

"My sympathy goes to the family of both Bert Whalley and Roger Byrne in their tragic loss and I feel too for the rest of those connected with the club who have suffered a severe blow. I knew them all – they were my friends."

It was not only the ambitions of Manchester United

which were thwarted by the tragic events at Munich. England's forthcoming World Cup hopes also suffered a blow with the loss of the established international trio of Roger, Tommy Taylor and Duncan Edwards, along with those on the fringe of the squad like David Pegg and Eddie Colman.

England's international manager at that time, Walter Winterbottom, was a great admirer of Roger's and the years have not diminished his admiration, as shown in the following tribute.

"Before the Munich disaster, Roger Byrne, Tommy Taylor and Duncan Edwards of Manchester United, were established players in the England team which was confidently looking forward to success in the World Cup Final competition in Sweden, having beaten West Germany, the World Cup champions of 1954 in Berlin and also Brazil at Wembley. The loss of these three players – the spine of the England team – was a grave blow to England's prospects, as all three players were outstanding.

"Roger Byrne, the captain of the young Manchester United side, was gifted with strong qualities of leadership and self-assurance which were bolstered by his constant high standards of play at left back. Having at one time played in the left wing position, Roger was fleet of foot and was rarely outpaced when defending. He had also a sound tactical awareness which enabled him to encourage other players to give their best in combined play. His own short passing game was accurate and his long passes often found their mark leading to goal-scoring opportunities.

"Roger had a cheerful demeanour, which readily attracted warm friendship from players and officials. After he was first capped for England in the match against Scotland in 1953-54, Roger became a regular international at left back with many outstanding displays. One of his best coming in the 7-2 victory against Scotland at Wembley on April 2nd 1955.

"Personally I held Roger in high esteem, not solely as a good player but as a man. He was a fine example for young players to emulate and I was immensely grieved that he should die so tragically in the prime of life."

Bill Foulkes was one of those fortunate to be spared in the disaster and took over as captain from Roger in the immediate aftermath. Time has not quelled Bill's admiration for his former teammate and he was quick to add to the tributes.

"At United, Roger and I were amongst the oldest, but I was not one of his "group", partly due to the fact that I was, as I said before, a part-timer. Roger would hang around with the likes of Don Gibson and Tommy McNulty.

"I partnered Roger on many occasions at full back and we enjoyed some great times. He was an extremely nice person to know and would have captained United not only to the European Cup but also the League and FA Cup double if it had not been for Munich, such was the potential of that team. I even think we would have emulated Real Madrid.

"You read that Roger was an average player, which was true, but he read the game better than most and used his brain well. Although studying physiotherapy, he wanted to stay in the game in this capacity and would have probably stayed with United. He was a superb captain and a superb person."

Another who was quick to pay tribute was a man who had a big influence on Roger's footballing career, former United captain Johnny Carey. The soft-spoken Irishman said at the time: "Roger, the gay cavalier, with tremendous emotion beneath the thin veneer of imperturbability, the supreme confidence that came from him, knowing that he could give any winger a couple of yards start in twenty.

"A modest captain, a future captain of England and a

man who was kind enough to say that I taught him something even when he was a full England player."

On the afternoon of Wednesday February 12th 1958, the streets around the Parish Church of St. Michael's, Flixton, were lined with men, women and children, who had left household chores undone, took an hour off work or an afternoon off school to pay their respects to United's captain. Many stood on walls for a better vantage point, while others crowded into the grounds of the church.

Men stood bareheaded in working clothes ready to return to their employment after the funeral, while women huddled together, some comforting children in prams, as they dabbed their eyes with their handkerchiefs.

In complete silence they watched the arrival of United chairman Harold Hardman, assistant manager Jimmy Murphy and acting secretary Les Olive. Former United captain Johnny Carey, now manager of Blackburn Rovers, and England team boss Walter Winterbottom. Representatives from Manchester City, including Dave Ewing, Roy Little, Ken Branagan and Joe Hayes along with many other familiar faces. There were also nurses from the hospital where Roger did his physiotherapy course.

Three cars loaded with flowers preceded the hearse, and as the church clock struck quarter-past three, the coffin was borne into the grounds and sobs could be quite clearly heard from the waiting crowds, as Joy Byrne, accompanied by Roger's parents, other family members and friends, entered the already packed Church, where Football League referees acted as ushers.

During the solemn, moving service, the Rector, the Rev Peter Ettrick said of Roger: "He was a good man and a great sportsman. He was a true Britisher. He was a great leader. And because of his brilliant ability he became an international figure. But there was no fuss or palaver with him away from the game. He was just Roger Byrne, a friend of all.

From Triumph to Tragedy

"The boys looked on him as their boyhood hero. Many a lad will be sorrowing today with his young wife and family."

Half an hour later the funeral procession emerged from the church and left for Manchester Crematorium. More than 30 cars followed along the route through Flixton, Urmston and Stretford where crowds lined the pavements.

Outside Simpson's Ready Foods factory workers stood three deep, while at the busy King Street-Edge Lane-Chester Road junction at Stretford, the traffic lights were stopped and police controlled the traffic and the large crowds who packed all corners of the streets.

Old Trafford stood only a short distance away, its stands and terraces never again to vibrate to the football of the Busby Babes. Cries of "Good ball 'Rog'" and "Well done Roger" would never be heard again. The legend was now a memory.

LIFE MUST GO ON

The dark shadow cast by the tragedy at Munich hung over Manchester for quite some time and, in the immediate aftermath of the crash, matters were particularly testing in the day-to-day running of the football club.

Matt Busby's assistant, Jimmy Murphy, had missed the trip to Belgrade, as he was also the Welsh international team manager. He had been involved in a World Cup qualifying fixture, against Israel in Cardiff, on the same day as the match in Belgrade.

Upon returning to Old Trafford the following afternoon, oblivious to the events at Munich, Murphy was deeply affected by the devastating news awaiting him. He now found himself in charge of team affairs, if 'team' was the correct word to use, with only a handful of experienced players and untried youngsters at his disposal.

The top of the table clash with Wolverhampton Wanderers at Old Trafford on Saturday February 8th was immediately postponed, as was the FA Cup tie against Sheffield Wednesday, scheduled for seven days later, giving Jimmy Murphy a little breathing space in which to put a team together.

Thirteen days after the crash, a solemn-faced Bill Foulkes led Jimmy Murphy's United out of the dank tunnel below the stand and onto the Old Trafford pitch to face Sheffield Wednesday in the postponed fifth round FA Cup tie in front of a highly emotional 59,848 crowd.

Not only did the rebuilt United overcome all odds to defeat Wednesday 3-0 and progress into the next round, they went all the way to the Final itself on a wave of national emotion, only to lose, in controversial circumstances, to Lancashire neighbours Bolton Wanderers 2-0.

If Jimmy Murphy had not been involved with Wales and had travelled to Yugoslavia with United, he may have suffered a similar fate to that of his friend Matt Busby or the youngsters he had helped nurture through the United ranks. The history of Manchester United might have taken on a completely different course.

It was not only Manchester United that had to pick itself up and continue as best it could in the circumstances. The families and friends of those who had died also had much to do as they began to rebuild their shattered lives.

For Joy Byrne, the events of Thursday February 6th brought her life to a shattering halt, with the days that followed little more than a daze.

"I did not read a newspaper for days, maybe weeks after the crash," Joy confessed, "so I had no idea what was being reported or how the press were handling the accident. The item in the early editions of the *Manchester Evening Chronicle* relating to Roger supposedly having survived was therefore never seen and it was something I was completely unaware of up until recently.

"A number of the wives went over to Germany in the

days following the crash," continued Joy, "but I decided not to. United obviously offered me the opportunity to do so, but I declined their invitation.

"The funerals were delayed a week, which did not help, as it took that long to get the bodies back home. During that week and for some time afterwards, there was a constant stream of friends and visitors to the house, all of whom were very very kind. Amongst the visitors were numerous religious representatives, the Lord Mayor of Manchester, the Mayor of Stretford and obviously people from United, including Louis Edwards, who had recently become involved at board level.

"After the crash I also received over 1,000 letters of condolence, not just from people in this country, but from people all over the world. Many were addressed simply – 'Mrs Roger Byrne, Manchester, England'.

"To be honest, I do not know how long it took for me to get over Roger's death. Roger's dog, Sandy, certainly knew something had happened, as he pined for three weeks before dying of a broken heart.

"Expecting a baby, something that Roger was completely unaware of, was a great comfort and I seem to have blotted out the time from the crash until Roger jnr was born in October 1958. I had a 40-week pregnancy, with Roger jnr being born 38 weeks after the crash.

"Thankfully, I had plenty of support in those testing times from friends and family alike. Tom Gilmour, a close friend of Roger's was particularly kind and I remember him taking me round to visit Jean Busby to enquire about Matt. I remember also the first time I saw Matt again following his return home from the Munich hospital. It was a very sad, emotional and moving meeting for us both."

Joy is quick to praise United for their help in the days and years that followed. "Les Olive, in particular, was very kind after the crash," she said, "and the club have always treated me very courteously. I have never asked anything of them and never expected anything. They have always been extremely friendly on all occasions and I have only good to say about the directors and staff.

"Roger jnr and I were invited to the 1968 European Cup Final, but we had unfortunately already planned to go on holiday to Tunisia. We did, however, watch the match along with a few other British holidaymakers. Sadly for Roger, he also had to miss the 1999 Final in Barcelona through illness."

"I do not seek personal contact with United, there is no reason to do so. However, since Roger has been ill, Ken Merrett rings from time-to-time to check on his progress. Ken has also been very accommodating to Roger whenever there is a request for tickets etc."

Did Joy ever consider distancing herself from the game and the club which held so many memories for her? "No, definitely not. It never really occurred to me to do so, although it was around nine years before I did return to Old Trafford to watch a game. To be honest, it didn't bother me, nor did it feel strange returning for that first time, as it was a completely different team of players. When Roger jnr. became a ball boy, I would attend every home match, first team or reserve. Today, we have season tickets and I still enjoy the game as I always have done."

In February 1974, Joy and her son left the family home in Flixton and moved to Northenden, following her marriage to James Worth, an English teacher at William Hulme's Grammar School, where the youngster was a pupil. Three years later, James took up a teaching appointment in the Lake District, where the couple still live today.

Each February, the memories surface, but February 1998 produced more media attention than most of the previous years as the club decided to commemorate the fortieth anniversary of the disaster with a special service in Manchester Cathedral and a Memorial match at Old Trafford.

The Memorial Service, held on February 6th, was a

Roger Byrne - Captain of the Busby Babes

poignant, moving evening for everyone in attendance and must have been more so for those with a personal involvement. "I thought the Service was perfect in every way," said Joy. "It was reverent without being depressing. Knowledgeable people said wonderful things about the talented players and staff of United and also the newspapermen who died. We were sitting with the other relatives at the front of the Cathedral and I lit one of the candles during the service.

"Over the years, I had seen most of the other relatives and the survivors from time to time, so there was no stress or strain in meeting up again. The following day's League match against Bolton was also an immensely enjoyable and memorable afternoon.

"As for the Memorial Match, we all attended, and again thoroughly enjoyed the occasion. It was great entertainment, not in the football sense, but in the fun sense. Many felt that it was more about Eric Cantona than the memory of Munich, but I felt that Cantona added to the entertainment which was what the evening was all about."

Village life in the Lake District is a far cry from the hustle and bustle of Manchester, but it has provided Joy and James Worth with the perfect home for the past twenty-odd years, a home also shared by a daughter, born a couple of years after moving there.

One or two of Roger's United trophies stand rather inconspicuously in the lounge of the family home, while in the drive, Joy's car carries the number plate which adorned Roger's Morris-Minor all those years ago.

Being the wife of a famous footballer over four decades ago was vastly different from that of today, but it was a role Joy Worth enjoyed. It was a life which brought her many friends and memories, a life which changed dramatically one cold February afternoon.

Appendix 1 - Roger Byrne Jnr

Roger Byrne jnr was born 38 weeks after the Munich Air Disaster and from an early age he was aware of who his father was and what he had achieved as a footballer with Manchester United and England. This was mainly due to his grandparents, Roger's mother and father, to whom he was very close. In particular, Roger's father was always eager to recall incidents from his son's football career.

"As a youngster living in Manchester I was quick to pick up on the history of Manchester United and of course my father's part in their success during the 1950's," says Roger jnr. "There was always considerable media interest in my mum and I, especially when February came around, with reporters from local and national newspapers often turning up unannounced on the doorstep in the hope of an interview. Prior to the 25th anniversary of the disaster in 1983, the Daily Mail arranged for me to fly to Munich and visit the site of the crash at the airport.

"With it having happened so long ago I did not think

that the visit would affect me too much, but on arrival at the site I became quite emotional. I also remember to this day the cold weather in Munich and thinking how awful it must have been on the day it all happened."

In the interview the Daily Mail carried at the time, Roger jnr said: "I thought I had come to terms with never having known my father, but being there, where he died so young and so tragically, I really choked. My emotions welled up inside and I felt particularly close to him. I was glad that I had at last been able to see where it had happened and it was like putting the last piece into a jigsaw puzzle. It completed the picture of my life. Coming here is a special moment for me. After all, I am just a few years younger than my father was when he died."

Many young boys are eager to follow in their father's footsteps with their chosen profession and Roger jnr was no different. "As with most young Mancunians I dreamt of becoming a professional footballer, with United of course, but from an early age I realised that unfortunately I was not going to make the grade. When I made the step up from primary to secondary school I went to William Hulme's Grammar School in Whalley Range where they played rugby as the main sport. So, my footballing ambitions really took a downward turn and more or less came to an end.

"Obviously, as a football-loving youngster I supported United and I can first remember visiting Old Trafford during season 1966-67, with my grandfather Bill Byrne, who was, of course, an avid supporter and who obtained a lot of enjoyment from taking me to games. I must admit, however, that I used to go alternate Saturdays to Maine Road with a friend of the family. City were doing well at this time and I enjoyed a feast of football at weekends.

"In 1968, my interest in United had developed so much that I decided to write to Matt Busby and ask if there was any possibility of becoming a ball boy at Old Trafford. His reply was eagerly awaited and much to my delight I was accepted. I used to be there for every game, first team and reserves, loving every minute of it. It was a sad day when I had to retire after three seasons at the age of twelve!

"Being a ball boy was a very special time for me, providing me with the opportunity to tread in my father's footsteps so to speak and also come face to face with people who were on the plane that fateful afternoon and who had shared part of my father's life. People such as Matt Busby, Bobby Charlton, Bill Foulkes and Harry Gregg.

"Upon leaving grammar school I moved to Liverpool Polytechnic, where I took a degree in sports science. I later became assistant manager at Huncoat Leisure Centre and am now working with Swindon Borough Council as a Recreation Manager in charge of Leisure Centres in Swindon.

"Most of my father's footballing items are on permanent loan to United, predominantly for insurance purposes, and on display in the museum, although I do have one of his international caps and a Brazilian jersey he swapped with an opponent. I believe that having his medals and other items on display in the United museum will help preserve his memory and those of his teammates.

"I doubt, however, if the memories of the players who died will ever fade, as the events of the 40th anniversary of the disaster clearly proved to me. The number of people both inside and outside Manchester Cathedral amazed me that night. The event was superbly organised and orchestrated in both a tasteful and professional manner. The tributes by the players and journalists were both moving and a great tribute to the club. Personally, I found the evening very difficult and I was sitting beside Ray Wood, who was crying with me at times during the service.

"The match against Bolton Wanderers the following afternoon was one of the most amazing moments of my

Roger Byrne - Captain of the Busby Babes

life, walking onto the Old Trafford pitch, laying the wreath and the perfectly observed minutes silence was a great tribute to Munich players and the fans of both clubs. Today, I am a United season ticket holder and still as passionate about United as ever."

Over the years Roger Byrne jnr has watched the likes of Best (his hero), Law, Robson, Cantona and Beckham enthral the thousands with their skills, but from time-to-time visions of another red-shirted hero appears, drifting across the green Old Trafford sward. This was one outstanding individual he never had the privilege of watching, but a player who was a legend like the players above in both Roger's eyes and those of all who saw him. His name? Roger Byrne.

APPENDIX 2 -

THE IMPORTANCE OF THE BABES

Although it is now some forty-odd years since that fateful afternoon in Germany, the name of Roger Byrne and those of his teammates live on.

Perhaps Duncan Edwards is more fondly remembered for his youthful enthusiasm and unfulfilled potential, but Roger was the captain of that marvellous mid-fifties side, who captured the imagination of all who saw or read about them. He was an inspiration to all and respected by anyone who came into contact with him. He still had a long playing career in front of him at both club and international level. He would undoubtedly have led both to numerous successes.

Permanent memorials to Roger and his teammates who died at Munich can be found in the Newton Heath area of Manchester, not far from the site of the club's old home in what was North Road. There you will see Roger Byrne Close, alongside other Walks and Closes named after the other lads who lost their lives.

Across the city, in the more familiar surroundings of Old Trafford, the Munich Memorial plaque outside the stadium, now so different from the Old Trafford of the 1950's, stands as a permanent reminder of those whose careers came to an end on February 6th 1958.

Inside the North Stand, in the club museum, Roger's contribution to United's history is noted by the inclusion in a special 'Legends' area, where items from his playing career are on display alongside similar bits and pieces relating to the likes of Meredith, Cantona, Robson, Law and Edwards.

The name of Roger Byrne could not appear anywhere else as he certainly was a legend, one of the Manchester United all-time greats.

APPENDIX 3
STATISTICAL RECORD

DATE OF BIRTH   8.9.1929

DIED   6.2.1958

MANCHESTER UNITED CAREER

Signed Amateur Forms   18.8.1948 (Club)
Signed Professional   4.3.1949 (Club)
                      7.3.1949 (League)

Roger Byrne - Captain of the Busby Babes
Central League Record

DEBUT: v EVERTON (AWAY) 9.4.1949
HOME DEBUT: v BOLTON WANDERERS 15.4.1949

	APPS	GOALS
1948-49	4	-
1949-50	28	2
1950-51	31	4
1951-52	16	5
1952-53	2	1

Positional Breakdown

1948-49	4	AT LEFT HALF	(No.6)
1949-50	12	AT LEFT HALF	(No.6)
	11	AT OUTSIDE LEFT	(No.11)
	5	AT LEFT BACK	(No.3).
1950-51	1	AT LEFT HALF	(No.6)
	12	AT OUTSIDE LEFT	(No.11)
	18	AT LEFT BACK	(No.3).
1951-52	3	AT OUTSIDE LEFT	(No.11)
	13	AT LEFT BACK	(No.11)
1952-53	1	AT INSIDE LEFT	(No.10)
	1	AT LEFT BACK	(No.11).

Lancashire Senior Cup

	APPS	GOALS
1949-50	1	-
1950-51	5	-

162

Statistical Record
Positional Breakdown

1949-50	1	AT CENTRE FORWARD	(No.9)
1950-51	1	AT OUTSIDE LEFT	(No.11)
	4	AT LEFT BACK	(No.3)

Manchester Senior Cup.

	APPS	GOALS
1949-50	1	-
1950-51	1	-

Positional Breakdown

1949-50	AT OUTSIDE LEFT	(No.11)
1950-51	AT LEFT BACK	(No.3)

FOOTBALL LEAGUE RECORD

	APPS	GOALS
1951-52	24	7
1952-53	40	2
1953-54	41	3
1954-55	39	2
1955-56	39	3
1956-57	36	-
1957-58	26	-

Roger Byrne - Captain of the Busby Babes
Positional breakdown

1951-52	18	AT LEFT BACK	(No.3)
	6	AT OUTSIDE LEFT	(No.11)
1952-53	33	AT LEFT BACK	(No.3)
	7	AT OUTSIDE LEFT	(No.11)
1953-54	40	AT LEFT BACK	(No.3)
	1	AT INSIDE RIGHT	(No.8)
1954-55	ALL	AT LEFT BACK	(No.3)
1955-56	38	AT LEFT BACK	(No.3)
	1	AT RIGHT BACK	(No.2)
1956-57	34	AT LEFT BACK	(No.3)
	2	AT RIGHT BACK	(No.2)
1957-58	ALL	AT LEFT BACK	(No.3)

FA Cup Record

	APPS	GOALS
1951-52	1	-
1952-53	4	1
1953-54	1	-
1954-55	3	-
1955-56	1	-
1956-57	6	1
1957-58	2	-

Positional Breakdown

ALL FA CUP APPEARANCES AT LEFT BACK (No.3)

164

Statistical Record
European Cup Record

	APPS	GOALS
1956-57	8	-
1957-58	6	-

ALL EUROPEAN CUP APPEARANCES AT LEFT BACK
(No.3).

International Record

FULL INTERNATIONAL CAPS	33
'B' INTERNATIONAL CAPS	2
INTER LEAGUE CAPS	6